RESTORING BRILLIANCE

BERNARD FRANKLIN, PH.D

Restoring Brilliance
by Dr. Bernard Franklin

ISBN 978-1-63360-331-8

For Worldwide Distribution
Printed in the U.S.A.

Urban Press
PO Box 5044
Williamsburg, VA 15221-0881
757.808.5776
www.urbanpress.us

CONTENTS

PREFACE

Everyone has a story and these stories are important because they help us understand ourselves and the world around us. Often, we focus on negative stories, which can lead to inaction, fear, anxiety, and depression. These negative stories are usually incomplete and distorted, but they nevertheless affect our mental and physical health. Sharing stories—even the negative ones—can connect us with ourselves and others, offer hope, and pass on a sense of identity. It's important to transform our pain through storytelling to avoid transmitting it to others, especially the next generation.

In this book, I will tell my story.

This book is my journey of healing and transformation, which is ongoing. It explores my experiences with anxiety, depression, and suffering, and how they found value and beauty in my journey. Throughout this book I emphasize the importance of embracing what is spiritual, being curious, and trusting the process of healing. Furthermore, I discuss the impact of trauma on the brain and body, and the need for knowledge and understanding to overcome trauma. Along the way, I will share insights and tools that have helped me on my journey, and encourage you to be open to new knowledge and experiences so you can be aware of your own journey and how to find freedom.

I am writing for all people, but my primary focus is on justice involved youth, incarcerated adults, or those transitioning out, for their families and their larger communities who have no standing, are on the bottom rung of life, and who live day to day without access to mental and emotional health care.

What if I told you that you are living beneath your privilege? You were not meant to think that you might die at 18 or 19 or 24. You were not put on the earth to spend the rest of your life behind bars. In you is a brilliance that maybe no one has ever helped you understand. You are not a piece of trash. You are not a waste or a human to be discarded. You may have the skills to solve a major health issues like sickle cell anemia or a cure for cancer. You are brilliant beyond your current knowledge. And that's what this book is about, restoring your brilliance. Your brilliance might be lost, stolen or have strayed. But if you read this book and then make a commitment when you're finished to follow some guidelines I propose, your brilliance can be restored and released.

This is coming from a man who was told by his minister during he and his wife's marriage counseling that he should be hopelessly hooked on drugs or alcohol, in prison, or dead from my childhood experiences. This is a story about how I restored my brilliance and am now able to give it back to the world around me. This is my story to encourage and inspire you to think and believe that you can recover and restore your brilliance.

You see, the pain that you and I have shared was not meant to destroy us. The environment you live in does not have to be permanent. That cell block you are in may not be permanent. What you thought may have been meant to harm you may be the very thing to make you stronger and more determined to reach your goals.

As Bryan Stpehenson says, you are not your worst mistake. You are the brilliance that is yet to unfold. I cannot wait to hear your story of restored brilliance.

The pain we don't transform we will transmit to others. The painful story we won't transform or redeem will ultimately be transmitted, and the wounds and ramifications will spew forth into the world around us. As Father Richard Rohr said, "Pain that is not transformed gets transmitted. If we do not transform our pain, we will most assuredly transmit it—usually to those closest to us: our family, our neighbors, our co-workers, and, invariably, the most vulnerable, our children."

Brilliance is a celebration of intellectual curiosity, creativity, and the pursuit of knowledge. Brilliance reflects themes of inspiration, innovation, and the beauty of ideas. We were all born with brilliance. But for some of us, our brilliance got lost, stolen, or it remained dormant. I hope this book helps you dig into your story to begin to explore and see your brilliance emerge. I hope you become eager to explore your life, your thoughts, and begin to see how you can use your brilliance to contribute to the world around you. Your brilliance was not made to shine alone or to impact only a few people.

By examining and then owning your brilliance, you will find motivation to embrace your deep inner passions and foster the special creativity that's only yours. I hope my story and this book serve as reminders that the journey to brilliance leads to immense personal growth and fulfillment.

I invite you to join me on this journey to brilliance by exploring how individuals and families heal through personal and spiritual practices as verified through modern brain and neuroscience research. Let me start with two true stories rooted in this country's sordid racial history that can demonstrate how someone's brilliance can be lost, stolen, or tarnished.

"White Mob in Tulsa Destroys Black Community; Kills Hundreds"

That was the headline on June 1, 1921, when the Black community of Tulsa, Oklahoma was left in ruins following several days of violent attacks by white mobs outraged that Black residents had organized to protect a Black man from lynching. Here is the background.

Tulsa's Greenwood District, known as the "Negro Wall Street," was considered one of the wealthiest Black communities in the nation in 1921. Many residents worked and did business in central Tulsa, meeting white men and women—some of whom resented their prosperity.

On May 30, while working in a building in downtown Tulsa, 19-year-old Dick Rowland boarded an elevator operated by Sarah Page, a 17-year-old white girl. When a store clerk heard a scream, he ran to the elevator to help Ms. Page and see if the young Black man in the elevator had tried to attack her. He called police and had young Rowland arrested.

Ms. Page told police that Mr. Rowland had startled her by touching her arm but insisted she did not want to press charges. Rumors soon spread, however, and turned into a sensationalized allegation that Dick Rowland had attempted to rape the young woman. Police arrested Mr. Rowland at his Greenwood home and jailed him at the courthouse. The next night, a mob of white men gathered at the jail seeking to lynch him, but 30 armed Black men from Greenwood were there to ensure that the sheriff and deputies were able to protect Dick Rowland from that fate.

Enraged, members of the mob returned with firearms, and several white people were killed or wounded in the ensuing gunfight. When the Black men returned to Greenwood, white rioters followed and attacked the community, burning 40 city blocks, killing hundreds of Black residents, and displacing many more.

"In all of my experience I have never witnessed such scenes as prevailed in this city when I arrived at the height of the rioting," a military official recalled days later in a *New York Times* article. "Twenty-five thousand whites, armed to the teeth, were raging the city in utter and ruthless defiance of every concept of law and righteousness. Motor cars, bristling with guns, swept through the city, their occupants firing at will." Some researchers estimate that as many as 300 Black people were killed in the violence.

None of the white rioters were convicted of any crime for their violent attack, and survivors of the violence received no compensation for lost property. In 2001, 80 years after the massacre, Oklahoma approved funds to redevelop the area and build a memorial. Today, the Greenwood Cultural Center stands in the same community where the massacre took place, committed to preserving and sharing the proud and tragic history of "Black Wall Street."

A Georgia Mob

(Warning: this story includes graphic details of an execution and subsequent mutilation.)

On April 27, 1899, a white Georgia mob lynched a man for "talking too much about another lynching." After the man was turned over to authorities, the mob seized him and staged a brutal public lynching before a crowd of thousands of white people. The mob chained him to a tree, dismembered and mutilated his body as he screamed in agony, and then set him on fire while he was still alive. Afterward, residents fought over his remains, and some reportedly claimed pieces of his bones and organs as "souvenirs." Black sociologist and activist W. E. B. Du Bois later angrily reported seeing the man's severed knuckles on display in an Atlanta store window after the lynching. (History of Racial Injustice, Equal Justice Initiative, Montgomery, AL.)

People today say, "Just get over it. That's in the past. And we had nothing to do with what happened back then." I share these stories because the trauma from events like the two I just shared lingers for generations. It has become part of a collective subconscious that cannot be forgotten or overcome without engaging a transformative process that brings healing.

This book is dedicated to the many men and women whose stories we do not know today and whose stories will never be known. Yet their untold and unresolved pain lives on in the minds of generations that were yet to come. I dedicate this book to you. May you find rest in peace!

Dr. Bernard Franklin
Boston, MA
December 2025

P.S. There are many words and phrases in this book you may have never heard before. I have attempted to define them when possible. But you can always conduct a Google search to look up a word or phrase to see what it means. Don't be afraid to dive deep into new things and learning. Restoring your brilliance depends on your curiosity. Go for it!

INTRODUCTION

GENERATIONAL TRAUMA

Before I get to my story, let me frame this book's contents with what I have learned about intergenerational trauma and pain and what we know of how it impacts the behavior and mental wellness of present *and* future generations. I can't accurately share my story without first providing this context. Otherwise, my story could easily identify my mother, father, and family as dysfunctional or inadequate parents. While there were major issues in my family (isn't there in every family?), blaming it all on my parents would not tell the full story.

I want to do them justice and share as much of the background as I can to help us all understand how important it is to take care of our stories today. Some of us cannot move on and restore our brilliance until we know and understand as much as possible about our past. We cannot allow the forces around us to discount this historical information as nonsense or irrelevant. There are major consequences from some of the events like I described in the Introduction that we can no longer deny or ignore. I refuse to tell my story in ways that could seem to belittle or shame my mom and dad.

Most of our systems that track human behavior like the criminal justice system, judges, lawyers, prosecutors, clergy, and human and mental health professionals primarily focus on the person in front of them. They only ask questions about their lifetime, which for the young does not represent a long period of time. Only recently have we begun to ask the question, "What happened to you?" The answers are important because the person standing before those officials are the sum of the deposits made by past generations for good or bad, positive or negative behavior. It is long past the time for us in the justice or healing professions to ask the questions, "What happened to you? How did you get here?"

Recent research suggests that traumatic experiences can have epigenetic effects, meaning they can influence gene expression without altering the underlying DNA sequence. The research further suggests that these changes may be passed down from generation to generation. In other words, trauma can have physical as well as emotional and mental implications. It can leave scars on the body as well as the psyche.

This phenomenon is particularly relevant to the study of populations with a history of profound trauma, such as Holocaust survivors, Native Americans, and descendants of those who experienced slavery, Jim Crow systems, and continued racism and despair—as well as the survivors of the Civil War. Each person has a story within a bigger story and to ignore the bigger story is to limit our effectiveness in healing the present by addressing the past—not to keep the past alive but to bring some kind of resolution. Let me give you some information that will help you understand why I singled out the groups who have experienced significant trauma and pain.

1. Holocaust survivors and descendants

Studies have shown that Holocaust survivors and their offspring may have epigenetic changes in their gene structure, which is associated with stress response and an increased risk of anxiety and other mental health disorders. Children of Holocaust survivors have been found to have lower levels of DNA methylation in certain genes compared to control groups.

One study found altered stress hormone profiles in descendants of these survivors, potentially predisposing them to anxiety disorders. Research on them and their children provides some of the first evidence in humans of epigenetic changes being passed down to offspring after a traumatic event.

2. Native Americans and descendants

Research on Alaska Natives has found associations between historical trauma and DNA methylation differences in genes related to stress response and health outcomes. Exposure to trauma and stressors, which are more common among populations with a history of historical trauma, can induce epigenetic modifications or changes in how their DNA, which does not change, can change its expression.This may contribute to poor health, according to a two-pathway model.

Epigenetics is how our family history, environment, behaviors, and lifestyle choices, like diet and exercise, changes how our genes work without altering the actual DNA pattern. Think of your DNA as a book of instructions; epigenetics adds bookmarks or sticky notes to certain pages, turning genes "on" or "off," affecting which proteins your cells make and how your body functions. These epigenetic changes can sometimes be passed down to future generations and are often reversible, unlike genetic mutations.

The study on Alaska Native communities also highlighted the importance of cultural identification and engagement with traditional practices as potential buffers against the effects of historical trauma and their epigenetic manifestations. Some research suggests that there might be inherited resilience in Native American populations that warrants further scientific investigation, according to researcher Joseph Gone.

3. Descendants of slavery and extreme racism survivors

Some researchers and activists propose that racial disparities in modern health and well-being can be linked to the trauma of slavery and its potential epigenetic transmission across generations. However, the scientific evidence for transgenerational epigenetic transmission of trauma in humans, particularly in the context of slavery, remains limited and is a topic of ongoing discussion and research.

Ongoing societal factors like racism and systemic oppression are considered more direct and probable contributors to present-day racial health disparities in African American communities. It's important to consider the potential reversibility of epigenetic modifications, suggesting that improvements in environmental conditions and targeted interventions could potentially mitigate trauma-induced epigenetic effects and improve health outcomes in affected communities.

4. Descendants of Civil War veterans

A study on the descendants of Union Army soldiers who were held as prisoners of war during the Civil War suggests that the sons of those who endured particularly harsh conditions were more likely to die younger compared to the sons of soldiers who were not prisoners. The researchers controlled for other factors and believed this effect on mortality may be linked to epigenetic changes passed down through generations.

A similar effect was noted in a study of a Swedish population where the paternal grandfather's experience of food abundance was linked to reduced longevity and increased risk of cardiovascular disease in his grandsons.

Important Considerations

Here are some things to keep in mind where trauma and its intergenerational effects are concerned:

- While research in this field is growing, it's essential to interpret findings with caution since epigenetics is a complex matter, and many interacting biological and environmental factors contribute to an individual's health and well-being.

- Epigenetics offers a new lens to understand the potential impact of historical and intergenerational trauma on health, and provides a framework for exploring potential interventions aimed at promoting resilience and healing.
- The concept of intergenerational trauma transmission through epigenetics is still actively being explored and debated within the scientific community

I have often heard discussions that only center around the sins *of* the ancestors, and not the sins done *to* the ancestors. In other words, people have tried to address the failures of people without addressing the failures perpetrated upon these people. Until recently, we have only focused on the sins of the parents and grandparents without taking into consideration that their behavior may have been the result of wrongs done to them that they may be passing on without resolution to their children and generations beyond.

However, more recent *psychological/sociological perspectives* are now addressing "generational trauma," showing how past experiences of hardship or trauma have affected individuals and families for generations. Generational trauma is the psychological term for trauma that is passed and shared from one generation to the next. This includes "historical trauma," which focuses on the accumulation of intergenerational trauma experienced by groups subjected to systemic oppression, like slavery or colonization.

Generational trauma can manifest as anxiety, depression, low self-esteem, difficulty forming attachments, substance abuse, or perpetuating unhealthy behaviors within families. Mechanisms for the transmission of generational trauma include:

1. *Epigenetics.* As we have already seen, changes in gene expression due to environmental factors like stress and trauma affect how future generations respond to stress.
2. *Family dynamics and parenting styles.* Unresolved parental trauma can influence parenting, creating unhealthy patterns in child-rearing.
3. *Cultural and social norms.* Trauma can become embedded in cultural norms, affecting a community's beliefs and behaviors.
4. *Environmental factors.* Ongoing environmental stressors, such as poverty or systemic oppression, can contribute to the perpetuation of trauma across generations.

Breaking the cycle of generational sin or trauma requires acknowledging these patterns and seeking support and treatment for healing and recovery. This can involve individual and family therapy, education, self-care practices, building supportive communities, and engaging in cultural connections.

This is the reason I seek to paint my story against this backdrop while encouraging others to do the same. With the knowledge we have today concerning trauma and brain science, we can move forward to a healthier lifestyle in a more informed fashion.

One more thing. This book seeks to show that healing from chronic trauma, no matter its origin, must incorporate the truth that humans are made up of three parts, which means we are comprised of body, mind (or soul), and spirit. The *body* refers to the physical, tangible aspect of a human being, including our physical form, organs, and senses. The *mind (or soul)* encompasses our thoughts, emotions, personality, and self-awareness. The *spirit* is often considered the core of our being, our essence, or our connection to something larger than ourselves, such as a higher power or the spiritual realm.

The core idea of a threefold nature emphasizes the interconnectedness and importance of all three for a complete and balanced human healing experience. Programs like the 12-step program in Alcoholics Anonymous recognize the threefold nature of addiction (body, mind, and spirit) as contributing to the disease. Without considering all three domains, there can be no complete, lasting healing.

This is a concept consistent with various philosophical and spiritual traditions and suggests that these three aspects are interconnected and contribute to the wholeness of a person. The complete healing from severe, complex trauma cannot occur in only one or two of these aspects. We must understand and embrace the truth that *all* our being is connected and integrated to the whole of the person—and all these parts are impacted for good or not-so-good as we experience life and all its challenges and opportunities.

Let's get started.

CHAPTER 1

MOM AND DAD

"In the depths of adversity, brilliance often emerges as a beacon of hope." – Zoe Carter

I was born on April 5, 1953, which was Easter Sunday morning, in Colored People's Hospital in Okmulgee, Oklahoma. I am the eldest of 7 children born to my parents. As of this writing, my father is still alive at 95 years old. However, my mother passed away at the age of 66. One of my brothers, who was two years younger than I, passed away in 2007. I have four surviving sisters and one brother. As the oldest of seven, Mom and Dad played a significant role in my emotional development, or lack thereof. Let me emphasize that I love my mother and father. I have come to appreciate my journey to where I am today—but it wasn't always that way.

My father, and my mother for that matter, gave me all they had. My dad's heritage or background is Caucasian (or White) and African

American; and my mother's heritage is Choctaw and African American. They were sharecroppers living in rural Oklahoma squalor. They said the white landowners were mean, cruel, and demanding. Their parents did not focus on how to create and sustain a system for a healthy family. In those difficult days for them it was all about survival while they picked cotton in the heat of the summer and then trying to survive the brutally cold winters. What they received or did not receive from their parents or family is what they shared or replicated with me and my siblings. I have grown and matured to be able to accept this truth.

Dad was the oldest of twelve children and was raised in an era right before the Great Depression, a harrowing period for many Black men. There was not an emphasis on raising a healthy family. Instead, it was all about survival. They were doing what they could to put enough food on the table and survive one more day. My dad's father did not give much to his family emotionally, and that's what my dad observed and learned.

Let me make an important point: I don't know much about our past family history. I now realize that I should have engaged my parents to obtain more family background information. I regret not doing so, for that past impacts me today with patterns, emotions, and feelings that I cannot explain and for which I do not have adequate background.

This is the case for many African Americans. We don't know our family history. We don't know why our parents lived and responded to life as they did. Some of the stories would be too brutal or shameful to discuss in a class or read in a book. But we can't move on without embracing and honoring (or at least acknowledging) the past. Our ancestors would want us to understand what they went through. Now I wish I could sit down with them and hear their stories and the intense pain that accompanied them.

Several years ago, I met Dr. Joy DeGruy at a conference in New Orleans. Dr. DeGruy is the author of *Post Traumatic Slave Syndrome: America's Legacy of Enduring Injury and Healing* (2005). Her book contends that the experience of slavery and the continued discrimination through Jim Crow systems and oppression endured by many African Americans created the intergenerational psychological trauma I mentioned earlier, leading to a psychological and behavioral syndrome that is common to many present-day African Americans. This behavior may manifest as a lack of self-esteem, persistent feelings of anger, and internalized racist beliefs. We had a significant albeit brief conversation during which I shared some of my story. While obviously she could not verify the truth of any part of my story, she commented that there could be many underlying truths that have impacted my lived reality today.

What I do know is that my grandfather and his family moved from the Dallas, Texas area in early 1900s. They migrated north to rural Oklahoma because the boll weevil had destroyed the cotton crop in rural Texas. My grandfather and his family probably left to scavenge for food and life's existence. There were perhaps other atrocities they had to endure but that would have been bad enough. They had no consistent work and what they could do led to subsistence living—today it would be called food insecurity. It used to be labeled hunger. So being left to scavenge could have meant that my grandfather's family had no safe family structure with love and security. He may not have been shown love. It was undoubtedly all about survival first and foremost.

My dad said his dad did not work but would make him work. In high school, Dad would get up early to start the fire in their coal stove at school so that it would be warm when the teachers and students arrived. Dad made a small amount of money, but his dad would take it from him to buy food and care for the family. Otherwise, Grandpa would roam the countryside looking for items to sell, sort of like eBay long before the Internet existed.

Dad said he left home the day after he graduated from high school to join the Army. He had to walk 40 miles to leave home and get away from his dad. He completed his miliary training in Maryland and went off to fight in the Korean War. When he talked about the war, he seemed to light up as if he enjoyed the Korean culture. He said the Korean women treated him and his African American solider buddies with warmth and respect—more respect than he said he received back home. He enjoyed it so much he returned home a heroin addict. Returning home addicted, he faced the added challenge of being opioid dependent. His behavior was not uncommon for miliary men dealing with life-and-death consequences of war in a foreign country.

Mom and Dad confirmed Dad's addiction.

Mom was sure that he was addicted when they married but went "cold turkey" to stop. They married in August 1952, and I was born in April 1953 on Easter Sunday. Mom said she was overjoyed to have given birth to her firstborn son on Easter Sunday.

Mom said I was a "colicky baby," which means I cried a lot. The worst of my crying was at night when Dad needed his sleep so he could get up the next day for work. Angry at the constant crying, and wanting Mom to comfort me, he often closed me up in a dresser drawer at night. The dresser drawer was my baby bassinet because they could not afford a real one.

Dad learned to be emotionally distant due to his own unresolved issues from how his dad raised him. I never heard Dad say "I love you" or pay much attention to me unless it was severe punishment. Today, this might be labeled Childhood Emotional Neglect (CEN). I don't have many lasting memories from my early childhood days. I may be suppressing some events and scenarios. Every now and then I get a faint glimpse of some event from my past, but it floats in but disappears.

I was born at a time when the notion of the family was structured, with authoritarian fathers believing they needed to take strict control of their children and use as much force as necessary to raise their children "right." With such a rigid philosophy on family and child rearing, those raised within its structure would often suffer abuse and either eventually rebel or learn to accept and perpetuate it, bearing the consequences emotionally and psychologically for the rest of their lives.

I didn't have many close friends while

growing up in our Pentecostal church. My parents believed that much of the world around us was evil and corrupt, so they sought to protect me from negative influences. Therefore, I grew up in isolation, never going to movies or high school dances until I was a junior in high school. When I went, I didn't, I couldn't, tell them I was going.

I grew up afraid of my dad. He was strict and rigid and any act of perceived disobedience was met with anger and rage. I developed an ulcer by age ten caused by my fear and anxiety. I felt he resented me, and I could not figure out why. I had a feeling deep down that he was angry with me because I had done something wrong. I tried to figure out what I had done to make him so angry.

My escape was reading and schoolwork. I found I could retreat to my bedroom to soothe my ulcer pain and to be alone because Dad's moods and negative behavior were unpredictable. I didn't share my pain with my parents, knowing it wouldn't receive any sympathy or comfort. Dad's punishments were severe, and I was hesitant to share that I was hurting because I was taught that boys needed to be strong and endure pain like a man.

Dad's instructions were often unclear. He yelled that I should go outside and pick up everything that didn't grow. At least then I found relief in getting out of the house but I was afraid I had misunderstood, and didn't really understand what he had told me to do. As an adult looking back, I see it might have been Dad's way of saying to get out of his sight. When he said pick up everything that doesn't grow, I stayed outside for hours, picking my leaves, tree branches, paper, bottles and everything lifeless.

I felt unwanted and unappreciated.

I was about ten years old when Dad said I would not get any Christmas gifts because they needed to get things for our growing family and for my younger brothers and sisters. He shared the decision like I was a little man, assuming I would understand that they had little money and had to skimp to make ends meet. I remember getting some underwear and socks after which I rushed off to my favorite place in the house—my bedroom. I would lie in bed thinking of how I was going to explain to my friends at school about those meager gifts when holiday break was over.

I can never forget the discipline he gave me. "Whippings" do not describe their pain and the humiliation. He would grab my pants and pull them tight so each strap of his belt would sting as much as possible. His "switch" was a ripe peach tree limb. The hard part was when I had to go outside and find one he would use on me, knowing that I was going to feel it.

One Sunday at church, I called a girl a "fool." When I arrived home, Dad asked me about it, which caught me off guard. As he questioned me, my anxiety kicked in big time. I simply could not remember what I had called her. Dad thought I was defying him by lying, but I truly could not remember. He took me into my bedroom, took off his belt, and beat me while asking what I called the girl. I could not cry. If I did, he would start all over or whip me harder. After what seemed like about 10-15 minutes of a major "beating," he stopped until after lunch. When the meal was over, he took me back to my room and started again. I still could not remember what I called the girl.

We all took a nap and then got up for Sunday evening service. After we came home from church, Dad asked me again if I remembered the word that I called the girl. I could not, so he beat me again more intensely, which at the time I didn't think was possible. After he maybe realized I was not playing games, he shared the word. I had called the girl a "fool," and that one forgotten word caused me more pain than anyone can imagine. I don't remember how I slept that night. I was humiliated after being beaten like that for most of the day in front of my siblings. That caused me to retreat even more into myself.

Where was Mom in all this? She was present as a stay-at-home mom, but Dad ruled the house. Mom had no opportunity to intervene, or she would not/could not intervene. Mom was a soul food gourmet cook before it was labeled soul food. Her fried chicken was not like anyone's I have ever tasted. Mashed potatoes were not packaged. Many weeks we had beans every night, but they were cooked with different seasonings so we didn't remember the night before we had also eaten red or white beans.

Her specialty was baking. Mom could bake cookies, pies, and cakes that were as good as her chicken. Usually there was always something sweet and yummy when we got home from school. After a beating, I could count on a treat to calm down my anxious nerves.

Mom knew I was suffering and the reason I

spent so much time in my bedroom. One day she took me to the doctor's office for an exam to see about my stomach ulcer. It didn't take the doctor long after asking me questions to turn to Mom and say, "This is stress related. No child has an ulcer at 12 from eating or some other issue. This is all stress." He went on to ask her something like, "What's going on in your house? You must get him out of there."

When we went back home, Mom mentioned to Dad that the doctor said I was under too much stress, but I never heard her say that he asked what was going on in our house that would cause their young son to develop an ulcer. Maybe she did not have the courage to say to Dad that "you are the source of our son's stress."

We never talked about it again.

What's a mother of many children with a high school education going to do if she left her husband in the early '60s? How would she take care of her children with her limited skills? During this time, most of Mom's friends cleaned the homes of wealthy white families. Mom did that for a while, but she had too much dignity to bow and nod to white people and clean their house. After several years of that hard work, she gave it up and returned home to clean and care for her own home. She kept sucking it up and stuffing it all down deep inside her being. She was smiling on the outside but crying on the inside.

As I got older, I lost myself in high school and working outside the house. I worked first as a cashier and bagging groceries. Then later in high school I worked at an upscale clothing store. It was an escape from the house for a couple of hours. Often on breaks I drank a quart of milk to soothe my stomach.

I was selected a commencement speaker for my high school graduation, which was a huge honor. I worked on my speech, polishing it and editing each word to make sure I spoke the sentiments of my neighborhood friends and family. When I was done, my African American history teacher was backstage to congratulate me. And of course, Mom was back there too. Everyone said I did a great job, except for Dad. I thought for once I really had done something he would be proud of and just maybe see himself in me. But I never heard from him until I went home. Then he put out his hand and said, "Nice job." I wanted more. I wanted a hug and to hear him say how proud he was of me. But he didn't have that in his repertoire of words.

I left the house to go to the graduation after party. I arrived at the dance, but I could not go inside. I stood outside and cried my eyes out in the parking lot. I never went in to the party to celebrate with my friends because I was so wounded and hurt. My hard work was about seeking Dad's approval and affirmation. Not getting it was more painful than any whipping or beating.

CHAPTER 1
MOM AND DAD

SUMMARY

- Our earliest experiences with parents and caregivers shape how we see ourselves and relate to others.
- Childhood memories—whether loving or painful—become part of our emotional wiring and influence how we handle trust and attachment later in life.
- Healing often begins by recognizing what was passed down to us and learning to process those experiences with honesty and grace.

REFLECTIONS

- • What are some of the strongest memories you have of your parents or early caregivers?
- • In what ways do you see their influence—positive or negative—showing up in your adult life?
- • What steps can you take to begin healing from any pain that traces back to those early years?

CHAPTER 2

MY COLLEGE DAYS

"Brilliance is the sweet fruit of curiosity, innovation, and unrelenting pursuit."
– Matthew Smith

I left home when I was 18 to attend Kansas State University. I knew I was never coming back home to live when I left. I was done with that chapter of my life.

While at the university, my workaholism took root as I sought approval through work and extracurricular activities. In my sophomore year, I was labeled an "overachiever" and for good reason. I was president of five organizations at the same time. When the yearbook came out, I remember thinking how nauseating it was to see me featured on two pages and labeled as a "leader." I wasn't leading, I was looking for approval and not giving myself the space I needed to heal my wounds. I gave my undergraduate years my all.

In my senior year, I ran for student body president and won as a write-in candidate against five candidates who were listed on the ballot. They were all white and I was the lone person of color. I worked night and day to convince the 15,000 students enrolled on campus to elect me as their president. Since I was a write-in candidate, the students had to write my name correctly on the ballot to vote for me.

That evening after dinner, I got a call from the staff. I thought the call would inform me that there would have to be a runoff and the top two vote getters would have to work another week to see who would receive a majority of the votes. Instead, the staff adviser introduced himself and said, "Bernard, you've won the election. You had more votes than all the candidates on the ballot with 55%. More students voted for you than all five candidates combined!" It took a minute to grasp the message. "Are you kidding me?" was my response. The staffer assured me he was not.

All the networks visited campus to question me and find out how a Black kid in the middle of the country made history as the first Black student president, not just at K-State, but in the country. I had to let all that sink in. Mom called, but I never heard from Dad. He didn't have the capacity to see himself in me. I had the brilliance that was never recognized by his father. And when someone has that kind of unfinished business, they pass it on and replicate it. They don't know any better.

After I graduated from K-State, I got married and we had a son. When that marriage began to fail, I found my way to Mobile, Alabama, and received my master's degree in counseling and behavioral studies from the University of South

Alabama (1989). In hindsight, this was my source of counseling I had needed and been looking for. It was there that I began to understand my father, my family system, my society, and myself.

It's interesting when I look back that I chose a degree in counseling. At that time, it was the only program of interest and the only one I could complete quickly since I was working for the university and had free tuition. Now I see how God used that master's program in ways I did not anticipate and would not have thought possible—but more on that later. Years later, I went back to Kansas State and earned a PhD in counseling and family studies, which capped it all off and brought much of my journey into focus. It gave me a firm foundation upon which I could build.

There is so much I could share. But I think you get the basic impression that my growing up was not pleasant or healthy. Parents often make mistakes with their first child because they did not take a class on parenting. And poor parents from dysfunctional backgrounds and systems that required survival skills rather than nurturing family skills pass that pain on to the next generation. It makes little sense to blame Dad for his lack of healthy parenting.

Naturally, I didn't have much of a relationship with him. I didn't know my father in a loving, fatherly way. I was the oldest growing up in a Pentecostal church (there will be more on that later as well). I never considered going to the streets or doing drugs or alcohol. My escape, my hope for the future, my sanctuary were classroom academic pursuits. Later, my escape and main personal expression was my work. My worldview required that I become more addicted to work, more addicted to school, and more addicted to academic process and progress.

Eventually, I sought the reasons, along with many other Black men, why we are so addicted to work or to anything for that matter—drugs, sports, opulent living, or leisure. Why have we lived this way? I am writing this book because I found some answers to those questions, and I want to share those life lessons and some of the rewards I've obtained from this process. These answers aren't just for Black males; they are for everyone and anyone, regardless of race or gender.

Now, on this side of my healing and wholeness, I've been asking myself, *What's the difference between one addiction and another*? After many years of reading, counseling, and teaching, I have found that an addiction to anything is just that—an addiction. We choose to put our energy, sometimes *all* our energy, into one place, practice, persona, or worldview to soothe or solve our anxiety or to be free from our low self-esteem. When we think that entity can help us, we devote ourselves to it, whether it's alcohol, drugs, religion, sports, or the pursuit of the American dream. Every one of us can give ourselves to things that in some ways don't really matter or even harmful, but that's what we do—and that's what I did.

CHAPTER 2
THE POWER OF ATTACHMENT

SUMMARY

- Secure attachment in childhood helps us form healthy relationships and manage stress throughout life.
- When attachment is disrupted—through neglect, trauma, or loss—it can lead to patterns of fear, mistrust, or avoidance that persist into adulthood.
- The good news is that attachment wounds can be repaired through consistent love, counseling, and safe connections with others.

REFLECTIONS

- How would you describe your ability to trust and connect with others today?
- Can you identify experiences that may have shaped your attachment style growing up?
- What relationships in your life now help you feel safe and valued, and how can you strengthen them?

CHAPTER 3

YOUNG ADULT YEARS

"To shine with brilliance is to recognize that failure is merely a step toward success."
– Ethan Brooks

I confessed in the previous chapter that I was addicted to work, so let me share some of the employment positions that consumed me and my time. For many years, I worked in higher education, starting at the University of South Alabama. Then I moved to Rollins College in Orlando, Florida, which was a great opportunity for me. From there, I returned to Kansas State to serve as assistant dean of students in 1990, and that's where and when I completed my PhD in counseling, higher education administration, and family studies (1996). After that, I moved to the National Center for Fathering, and one of my claims to fame is that I conducted a presentation on fathering for Marty Schottenheimer, who was then the coach of my beloved Kansas City Chiefs NFL team.

Marty was on his own journey, and some

of my story and background resonated with him. He asked me to serve as the team chaplain, which explains why I love the Chiefs as I do. I went to school in Kansas, but God used that team to help me realize what I was learning about myself was of value not just to me but to others. Unfortunately, I worked for the Chiefs before their recent success, so I don't have Super Bowl paraphernalia or a ring. It may seem like a big jump to go from the National Center for Fathering and the chaplain for the Chiefs to becoming a local church pastor, which is what I did.

I loved pastoring in partnership with my magnificent wife, Elsia, whom I married in 1987. I met her in Mobile, Alabama, where we got married and had our first child. Then we moved to Orlando in 1989, and from there went back to Kansas State in 1990, where we had two other children. Our son was born in 1991, and our daughter was adopted in 1995.

I had no intention of leaving the pastorate until an unexpected event occurred in our family. My wife was diagnosed with stage four breast cancer in 2000, and I needed to find a job with benefits that could cover her medical care. In 2002, I accepted a position with the Kauffman Foundation as vice president. Elsia, the love of my life and the finest woman I have ever met, passed away in 2005. Then, three years later, my younger brother died.

I found myself with a young family and life seemingly turned upside down. During this time, I was trying to apply all I had learned from my education to my own personal and emotional development, but it was a graduate degree earned from experience I would not wish on anyone.

From there, I became president of the urban campus of a five-campus community college from 2005 to 2010. I placed my daughter in a facility for young women in 2010 and I went off to obtain my trauma training at TCU. When she came back home in 2012, I chose to homeschool her rather than send her to a public or private school. She went back to finish her senior year about 2013, and I worked part-time for Kansas State and other places until I accepted a position at Mount St. Mary's in Maryland in 2018. In 2022, I attended a year-long program called the Leadership Fellowship at Harvard University. This program invited professionals to attend who were searching for what they wanted to do with the rest of their lives after they had enjoyed some career success. It was designed to be a year of rediscovering purpose and passion—and it certainly was for me.

It was during my time at Harvard that I began to understand how God was using my journey to help others. I didn't feel I was ready, but the people I was helping didn't seem to notice. They were drawing life and hope from what I was sharing. I tried to avoid the role, but God guided me back to it. As I write, I am managing director of Uncornered, a violence and gang reduction nonprofit that seeks to reduce gang violence and death. To say I never expected to be doing this is an understatement, but the work is urgent, and I have found a receptive audience for my message and wisdom.

My time at Harvard was valuable because it

gave me time to think and reflect. It was then and there that I began to understand why the leading cause of death for Black young men aged 14 through 25 is homicide. They're killing each other, which is no surprise if you pay attention to the news. It's so prevalent that we've become deaf and blind to its existence.

The second leading cause of death for Black boys ages 14 through 25 is suicide. They're not only killing one another; they are killing themselves. I was addicted to study and work; those were my escapes. There is no real difference between where they are now and where I was then. They are looking for answers, but their answers are fatal; mine kept me in the land of the living.

That issue and realization became my consuming passion during the twelve-month Harvard program. I began to ask myself how I can have an impact. I found myself organizing an urban gang summit in Boston. And then a friend of mine who was a college fraternity brother came to me one day and asked, "Bernard, there's a group launching a violence reduction program in Kansas City. Would you go have lunch with them?"

I went, and they were talking about the population I had just researched—Black men ages 14 to 25. I hope you can see God at work in this connection, for I certainly did—and still do. God had already formed and created a nonprofit to address that cause and problem without me having to do so. After Harvard, I joined the organization and was commissioned to design the support programs and garner the resources, which included mental health services and whatever other support we could give to get those who are willing off the streets and onto the path of healing.

At the end of June 2025, I "retired" from Uncornered and my time there was a powerful, important experience on my journey. This work helped me focus on how to give back and what to do after "retiring." My passion and purpose have always been to inspire people to reach their full brilliance. I can't give that purpose up now. I must find ways to disrupt and supplement our antiquated mental health system so it can better serve the poor and marginalized communities. To that end, I have started my own nonprofit named Restoring Brilliance.

Part of my worldview was developed in a church setting where I spent most of my childhood. Church was my father's attempt to protect us from the evil he perceived was on every corner, so if the church doors were open, we were there. I mention God not to convert you or have you identify with a church movement or theology. But I would be less than honest if I didn't mention that God factors into the healing and wholeness I am seeking for myself and the people I work with.

CHAPTER 3
THE DEVELOPMENTAL YEARS

SUMMARY

- Childhood and adolescence are seasons of rapid growth where identity, confidence, and worldview take shape.
- Positive reinforcement, stable routines, and emotional support build resilience; instability and criticism can leave lasting scars.
- Even if early years were difficult, new experiences and relationships can help reframe old beliefs and restore healthy self-esteem.

REFLECTIONS

- What words or messages did you hear most often growing up, and how have they shaped your self-image?
- Were there people in your youth who encouraged your strengths or helped you believe in yourself?
- How can you provide the kind of support and stability to others that you may have needed then?

CHAPTER 4

LEARNING TO SUPPORT MY DAUGHTER

"Brilliance is a light that, once ignited, can illuminate the darkest corners of the mind."
– Isabella Hart

When my wife passed away in January 2004, my four children and I were devastated. She was an incredible mother, wife, lover, friend, and lover of God. Her death impacted our daughter, the youngest of four. God brought her into our lives as a precious gift, fearfully and wonderfully made. I never realized when we adopted her that I would become her protector. But today, I embrace this role with reverence and awe.

Despite having three biological sons, I longed for the experience of caring for a daughter. This desire wasn't for spiritual reasons; it was simply a father's heartfelt wish. I didn't sense God directing me to adopt a little girl; I just wanted one.

Looking back, I see that God was instigating that desire all along. What I share now was part of His plan. Even though I thought it was a casual wish, God was indeed at work, bringing His plan to life. I am convinced that this book and its lessons are also part of His divine plan.

Wanting a little girl and so after some gentle nudging, my wife reluctantly agreed to visit a professional to discuss adoption. The representative from Catholic Charities was warm, gracious, and straightforward. After we shared our hearts, she explained that the adoption process required families to adopt the next available child, without choosing the gender. We decided to continue to try and have a daughter on our own.

About a year later, I received a call from the same social worker. It was a defining moment, one I will never forget. The call came on a Friday afternoon, the last day of my final exams at Kansas State, where I was working as the assistant dean of student life. The social worker asked if we were still interested in adopting a little girl. I said yes and promised to discuss it immediately with my wife.

The social worker shared the details of a young 16-year-old Caucasian girl from a small Kansas town who was pregnant to an 18-year-old African American man. The girl's father was furious and demanded she get an abortion or move out. Not believing in abortion, the scared teenager moved to Nebraska to live with family until the birth of her baby. She decided to give her baby up for adoption to an African American family.

The Kansas Catholic Charities social worker thought of us immediately. The young girl wanted an open adoption, where the birth parent and adoptive parents meet and share information, with the birth parent permitted to have supervised visitations. The social worker explained the benefits of an open adoption, and we agreed to proceed.

We put together our family story and pictures for the young mother. The next day, we drove to Nebraska to meet her. The circumstances of this young girl deeply touched my wife's heart. We shared our family story, and the young mother seemed comfortable with us. She said the baby was due in four weeks.

My wife began researching how a non-lactating mom could breastfeed an adopted baby. She learned that adoptive mothers could induce lactation using a breast pump. She purchased a pump and used it consistently for the remaining weeks. Her determination was inspiring.

Finally, the day arrived to pick up our baby girl. We drove to Catholic Charities nervous and anxious. The social worker placed the sobbing young mother with the baby girl in the center of the room. The young girl handed the baby to my wife, and we drove home.

My wife took to mothering this girl as if it had been her dream all along instead of mine. Our daughter grew and developed, knowing she was loved. The birth mother attended Kansas State University, and my wife supported her, creating a female mentoring and support system for her. In 1996, we moved to Kansas City, where I became vice president of the National Center for Fathering. We maintained contact with the birth mom, celebrating birthdays and other occasions together.

Then in April 2000, my wife was diagnosed with breast cancer. She had a mastectomy and several rounds of chemotherapy, and the cancer went into remission. In 2003, the cancer returned with a vengeance, spreading to my wife's liver, lungs, and brain. Despite the grim prognosis, my brave wife chose to trust in God for her healing and decided against further chemotherapy and radiation treatments. She was prepared to die if God did not heal her.

With her time limited, she had one request: to sit down with our daughter and share that her babysitter/nanny was in fact her biological mother. The conversation seemed to go well, but it was a lot for an eight-year-old girl to process. How does a child understand that one woman she thought was her mother is her adoptive mother and that woman is dying? And that the white woman who played with her, pushed her on her tricycle, and took her to McDonald's was really her biological mom?

I wanted to honor my wife's wish before her passing, but in hindsight, I regret granting permission. When my wife passed away, my eight-year-old daughter felt the pain of her death more intensely than did our three sons. About a year after her mom's death, she began to act out her fear and anxiety in destructive ways.

Within weeks of starting her sophomore year in high school, she was dismissed from her private high school. At the time, I was president of MCC Penn Valley Community College, an urban college facing many challenges. I immediately placed her in a local home for troubled girls.

After a few counseling sessions, her therapist advised me that my daughter needed her father to be more fully present. But what did that mean? Three months after her placement, I decided to resign as president of MCC Penn Valley. The College board was very generous, providing me with a year of salary and benefits.

The time away from the demanding 10-to-12-hour days as a community college president allowed me to delve deeper into the lives of wounded adopted and foster care children. I discovered that there was little support for families who adopt or foster children with deep emotional and psychological pain.

There is growing research around attachment disorder and brain development. I immersed myself in the training of the late Dr. Karyn Purvis at Texas Christian University's Institute of Child Development. I enrolled in her intensive training and became a certified attachment disorder instructor and provider. Dr. Purvis was a leading researcher on attachment disorder, brain development, and trauma-informed parenting and support for children of adoption and foster care.

I will never forget the first lecture of her intensive training. She said loudly and boldly, "The most dangerous place today for children is in utero [in the womb]!" I had never heard this. I interrupted her lecture to ask what she was talking about, for my training had always focused on children *after* they were born. None of my classes discussed the needs and challenges of the unborn child. She asked me to sit back, relax, and allow her to explain. She discussed how an anxious mom, a nervous mom, a mom who smoked, drank alcohol, or did any kind of drugs was sending those chemicals *and* emotions into her unborn baby. After that, she had my undivided attention.

I realized that our entire youth-serving culture would benefit greatly from this work, as many children, both urban and suburban, grow up without early secure and healthy attachments to their primary caregivers. My wife's death was a catalyst that opened my daughter's deep wounds which began in the womb of a young white girl whose father refused to accept that his daughter was carrying a mixed-race baby.

We have been misled to believe that children are resilient and can overcome their early childhood traumas. The truth is that for many, that trauma is buried deep in their brain and neurological systems, and any major event can trigger or reopen that wound. My daughter, like many hurting children, needed a loving caregiver to provide consistent discipline, not just after-school fun and games.

My daughter spent 13 months in the residential facility. When she returned home, I was a different father and caregiver. With my extensive training in attachment disorder, brain development, and trauma-informed parenting, I homeschooled her for her junior year of high school. I got her back on track, and she returned to public high school for her senior year. I carefully followed the Trust-Based Relationship Intervention principles and practices, specially creating a safe space without tension, anxiety, and my former raised voice. I also focused on nutrition, hydration (plenty of water), exercise, and a consistent daily routine. I could see her brain continuing to heal. She was less emotional, less belligerent, and more loving and caring. It was a daily process.

I did not give up on her. All my training and personal transformation served us well. She graduated with her class, which was quite an achievement. Those were tough days for a single father and a troubled young girl. We both learned and grew a lot from the experience. Today, she is a college graduate, living in northern Virginia and working in Washington DC.

I have discovered that looks are deceiving when evaluating someone's emotional health and stability. My daughter and I were both carrying trauma but someone observing us may not have picked up on the cues that we were. But let me stop with my story for now and focus on one specific aspect of what I have discovered, which is the study of neuroscience.

CHAPTER 4
TRAUMA AND THE BRAIN

SUMMARY

- Trauma changes the way the brain works, often keeping it in a constant state of alert and making safety or calm difficult to feel.
- When people experience repeated fear, neglect, or loss, the brain learns to survive rather than to trust or connect.
- Healing begins when the brain experiences new patterns—safety, predictability, love, and care—that help rewire old responses.

REFLECTIONS

- When you feel stressed or afraid, how does your body respond—tense muscles, racing thoughts, emotional withdrawal?
- How has past pain or fear influenced the way you think or react to others today?
- What practices or people help your mind and body feel safe and relaxed again?

CHAPTER 5

HIGH FUNCTIONING

"Brilliance thrives on curiosity; the more we know, the more we realize we can learn."
– Oliver Johnson

Let's talk about anxiety and stress in this chapter. Research indicates that a mild to moderate level of anxiety can effectively fuel someone's performance. Someone under stress preparing for a classroom exam studies to do well on the test. However, when the stress enters the overload stage, individuals must learn to cope. Some learn to do that better than others. "High functioning" is a term that describes individuals who perform well despite having to deal with serious conditions or significant life challenges.

For instance, a high-functioning alcoholic can manage to have a relatively normal life despite heavy alcohol use. Similarly, a drug addict might be termed high functioning if they handle life matters despite their addiction. This term neither minimizes their issues nor is it a formal diagnosis; rather, it describes someone who appears outwardly unaffected by their internal struggles. In the same sense, high-functioning anxiety refers to individuals living with anxiety while appearing to function reasonably well, though it is not a recognized mental health diagnosis.

Early pre-natal and childhood experiences certainly contribute to someone developing into a high-functioning individual with considerable anxiety. This coping strategy involves creating neuropathways that allow them to appear normal and successful, often referred to as a Type A personality. However, internally the individual experiences significant anxiety, which is masked by outward calmness.

Signs of High-Functioning Anxiety

High-functioning anxiety often propels an individual forward rather than rendering them inactive due to fear. Consequently, they appear successful in work and other responsibilities—arriving early, dressing impeccably, never missing deadlines. While they seem driven and successful, this facade masks underlying anxiety, which may not be known to family, friends, or colleagues.

Despite appearing capable and calm, the individual may struggle with substantial anxiety. They believe their coping behavior is normal and, fearing failure or disappointing others, they continue to unconsciously adapt. Characteristics associated with high-functioning anxiety include:

- An outgoing personality
- Punctuality

- Proactivity
- Organization
- High achievement
- Detail orientation
- Orderliness
- Activity
- Helpfulness
- Calm appearance
- Passion
- Loyalty

Challenges

An individual's success despite their high-functioning anxiety hides the struggle beneath. Anxiety drives their actions, sometimes making them appear difficult to read or constantly busy. Signs include:

- People pleasing
- Nervous habits
- Need for reassurance
- Procrastination followed by intense work periods
- Avoiding eye contact
- Overthinking past mistakes
- Inability to say no
- Insomnia
- Limited social life
- Comparing oneself to others
- Physical and mental fatigue
- Potential substance abuse

Known as overachievers, these individuals struggle daily with anxiety limiting their lives. They may achieve essential tasks but avoid activities outside their comfort zone, choosing to engage only those that calm their racing thoughts.

I was all of this. I was the high-performing individual driven by my lack of Dad's approval and emotional neglect; my brain and nervous system were activated by this overwhelming sense of anxiety. I had to learn to address the drive fueled by my anxiety and then adjust to a healthier balance between mental well-being and productivity. It took a major shift in my behavior that started with acknowledging that everything I have described in this chapter was me. This accurately defines how I was able to function as I did. As I recognized and accepted this, I delved into all I could find about the condition beyond what I have already described. Let me share with you more of what I found.

Types of Anxiety

The National Institutes of Mental Health identifies five major types of anxiety:

1. Generalized anxiety disorder (GAD)
2. Obsessive-compulsive disorder
3. Panic disorder
4. Post-traumatic stress disorder
5. Social anxiety disorder

Anxiety can stem from various causes, including:

- Stress at home
- Health issues

- Medication effects
- Abuse or neglect
- Bullying
- Loss of a loved one
- Relationship problems
- Divorce
- Financial issues
- Caregiver burnout

Understanding the source of one's anxiety may require professional assistance. About 20% of U.S. adults have an anxiety disorder, with some considering themselves high functioning. Help is available for all forms of anxiety, including high-functioning anxiety. However, characteristics of high-functioning anxiety may hinder seeking help because of the need to control their environment and activities.

Regular screening for anxiety is recommended for adults under 65. Effective treatments include cognitive-behavioral therapy (CBT), medications, mindfulness training, and other practices. Help is available, but I repeat that it starts with the recognition of the condition, which is a major step in recovery and treatment.

Coping With High-Functioning Anxiety

Here are self-help strategies I have discovered to help me reduce my anxiety:

1. Spend ten minutes daily on mental health.

2. Limit caffeine, maintain a healthy diet, stay hydrated, exercise regularly, and get enough sleep.
3. Stick to regular bedtimes and avoid staying in bed when your mind is racing.
4. Counter negative thoughts with realistic or helpful alternatives.
5. Adopt coping strategies for nervous habits, such as deep breathing or muscle relaxation.
6. Recognize that only the present moment exists.

I had to own that I had this condition and then to view my anxiety positively and not negatively to begin to overcome its stigma. And I deployed most of the strategies I just listed in my effort to overcome my anxiety.

A Personal Word

High-functioning anxiety can drive success, but it can also cost you your inner peace. Success does not need to stem from constant struggle. Sharing true feelings with a trusted confidante can lead to a more authentic experience of life. And most often you do not need to medicate to change your mindset as some professionals may recommend.

Stress is one thing, but trauma is an entirely different challenge as we will discuss in the next chapter where I will share my findings on the study and effects of trauma from neuroscience.

CHAPTER 5
THE ROLE OF RELATIONSHIPS IN HEALING

SUMMARY

- Relationships are one of the most powerful tools for healing emotional wounds—hurt caused in relationships can also be healed in them.
- Trust, empathy, and consistent care help re-wire the brain's belief that people are unsafe or unreliable.
- Healthy relationships don't erase the past but provide new experiences that teach stability, love, and belonging.

REFLECTIONS

- Who in your life today makes you feel genuinely seen and supported?
- What fears or habits sometimes make it difficult for you to open up to others?
- How can you practice building trust by being honest, dependable, and kind in your relationships?

CHAPTER 6

TRAUMA AND NEUROSCIENCE

"True brilliance emerges when you learn to laugh at the hurdles that life throws your way."
– Daniel Carter

The fields of psychology and mental wellness have not done an adequate job of bringing and applying the latest brain science research to the communities needing it most. Similarly, some parts of the faith and religious community refuse to fully embrace the science of the human body and brain. We accept and expect going to the moon and electric cars, yet we are hesitant to embrace the latest findings from the studies of brain science.

Some of my friends look at me skeptically when I share my passion and purpose for this topic. "I don't know about this brain science. It doesn't seem consistent with faith or theology. I don't see it in the Bible or the historic teaching of the Church," they may say. Understandably, we fear what we don't understand or fully know. If you fit into that category, I urge you to bear with me as I explain the latest and most significant research and findings about the science of the brain. I will do my best to keep it simple.

There aren't many easy-to-read books on scientifically researched brain science that top the *New York Times* best-seller list, but the book *The Body Keeps the Score* by psychiatrist and author Bessel van der Kolk did just that. This book is one of the most popular mental health books in the last decade, having sold two million copies worldwide. The numbers speak for themselves that this is a topic about which people are ready to learn more. It is one of the textbooks I use in the courses I teach on the connection between trauma and the brain. I have recommended the book to many people and keep extra copies to share with friends and family.

The Body Keeps the Score is a book of hope. Although it emphasizes the broad scope of traumatic experiences and the profound, often devastating impact trauma can have on an individual. It also makes the case that various forms of therapy are effective and that post-traumatic distress need not be a permanent condition.

In addition, Bessel van der Kolk included a summary of his four decades of experience studying the impact of trauma on the brain. His work represents a significant breakthrough in brain science, neuroscience, psychology, and body-centered therapies because he created a coherent blueprint for understanding and treating trauma.

Van der Kolk also helped us realize how common trauma is. According to his work, even if we haven't experienced it firsthand, there's a good chance we know someone with a history of trauma produced through neglect or abuse. That's what makes the material in his book so relevant and applicable for me and my work.

The Body Keeps the Score is not only to be considered a life-changing book for trauma survivors and mental wellness supporters, it can also help us become better parents, friends, teachers, coaches, supervisors, employees, partners, and faith/religious leaders. And who doesn't want that? I know his book will support you on your journey to become a kinder and more empathetic version of yourself as it did for me. Our journey through the book starts with a deeper understanding of trauma. Let me share and condense several of Van der Kolk's key lessons.

Lesson 1: The Brain-Body Connection Is Real

When we experience a real or perceived threat, it triggers our brain's alarm system. This alarm system, as Van der Kolk refers to it, involves the lower region of the brain called the amygdala, or the brain's smoke detector. The amygdala (pronounced uh-MIG-duh-luh), the almond-shaped part of our brain located at the bottom back area of our head, generates emotional responses and survival instincts. It helps us react to potential threats by triggering fear responses, but it is also involved in recognizing pleasure and rewards.

This brain region helps to code and store

memories of emotional events, making it essential for us to learn from past experiences. Understanding how the amygdala functions gives insights into various psychological conditions, including the anxiety disorders we are discussing, because it is quite involved in how we perceive and react to the world around us.

Understanding this intricate dance going on between different regions of our brain gives us a window into the challenges faced by individuals living with trauma. While the amygdala primes us for survival, it is the communication with the higher-order centers—especially the frontal lobes—that allows us to pause, reflect, and assess threats with greater clarity. In healthy circumstances, this collaboration ensures we don't remain trapped in a cycle of constant alarm. However, when trauma disrupts this balance, the brain's protective systems can become maladaptive, leading to persistent states of hypervigilance and emotional upheaval. It is in the interplay between these neural mechanisms that much of the struggle—and hope—for healing resides.

According to *The Body Keeps the Score*, the amygdala becomes hypersensitive after we experience a traumatic event. The unresolved event leaves a "code," a marker in the body and brain like a saved computer file or email. When the amygdala senses a threat (for example, a child senses harm from an adult in their house), it triggers or recruits the stress hormones and autonomic nervous system. This creates a whole-body response that propels the child to run, hide, fight, or on occasion freeze to confront the threat. In these moments, the child might experience a rapid heart rate, shallow breathing, sweating, and an inability to think clearly.

At the same time, Van der Kolk refers to our frontal lobes (the area of our brain in the upper front part of our head above our eyes) as the "watchtower." This area of the brain offers a view of the scene from above. In many cases, this area of the brain can help us process and better respond to a "false alarm," turning off the brain's smoke detector. With Post-Traumatic Stress Disorder (PTSD), however, the space between the amygdala and the frontal lobes shifts radically and quickly, making it much harder for the brain to recognize that the alarm is likely unwarranted.

As a result, these parts of our brains that are on the lookout for danger are *always* on alert. The slightest sign of a threat can trigger the amygdala and rush cortisol into our bodies and our brain. It is this overactivity that can keep us trapped in a prolonged state of emotional reactivity that can take its toll on the body. Our brains end up "marinating" in cortisol, damaging our brain function and neuro-system. In fact, according to *The Body Keeps the Score*, there are many examples connecting trauma to physical symptoms and health problems [see *5 Lessons We Learned* from *The Body Keeps The Score*, Myndrift.com]

Common responses to trauma include persistent fatigue, sleep disorders, nightmares, fear of recurrence, anxiety focused on flashbacks, depression, and avoidance of emotions, sensations, or activities that are remotely associated with the trauma. It's no surprise that untreated PTSD can lead to many mental health issues. Depression, anxiety, and substance abuse are common co-occurring disorders in individuals suffering from PTSD.

It should be noted that untreated PTSD has also been linked to chronic physical problems such as high blood pressure, high cholesterol, obesity, heart disease, chronic pain, fatigue, and decreased life expectancy. A person may not realize the connection between a traumatic event and their physical health symptoms, which helped me understand why there is so much illness in the African American and other marginalized communities. That's why untreated trauma has such deadly consequences.

Lesson 2: Trauma Causes Physical Symptoms

Being stuck in a prolonged state of emotional response or reactivity changes the way our body functions. According to Van der Kolk, when we are chronically angry or scared, constant muscle tension can lead to spasms, back pain, migraine headaches, fibromyalgia (widespread muscular-skeletal pain), and other forms of chronic pain.

To be aware of our responses to stress and our health, Van der Kolk recommends that we become curious. That means we begin to observe and learn how we are responding so we can develop healthy responses and physical reactions. This can occur when we practice mindfulness by sitting in quiet meditation and finding quiet spaces. Regularly practicing quiet moments calms down our nervous system, making us less likely to be thrown into fight-or-flight mode.

Practicing mindfulness means striving to be present and involved in whatever we are doing at the time. Some of the examples of quietness or mindfulness practices described in the book are forms of meditation, prayer, contemplation, and learning to live in the present moment, recognizing that yesterday and its troubles are gone, and tomorrow is not promised. All we really have is this present moment. And we should begin to embrace a sense of gratitude and stillness to simply be present in the now.

Mindfulness practice has been proven to positively affect numerous psychiatric and stress-related symptoms, including depression and chronic pain. It broadly impacts physical health, including improvements in our immune response, blood pressure, and cortisol levels. Learning to cut out the hyper-noisy culture we have created may be a challenge in the short term, but it pays dividends in the long term. A peace will come over you that even you can't imagine or fully understand.

I didn't understand it at first, but moments in my praise-and-worship-church culture triggered my anxiety after my mother, wife, and brother passed. I was under the impression that going to these spaces would help me, but they often left me more anxious and nervous. I have come to rely on being still and quiet as a remedy for my anxiety.

Lesson 3: The Mind Is Not Tending to the Present Moment

Being traumatized is not simply a challenge of being stuck in the past; it is also a big problem of not being fully present in the right here and now for healthy functioning. According to *The Body Keeps the Score*, as long as we don't resolve the trauma, the stress hormones that the body secretes to protect itself from danger keep circulating, and the defensive movements and emotional responses that belong to the past traumatic event keep getting replayed in the present—no matter how long ago the overwhelming event happened. We can remain in the space of stress and anxiety as if the event happened yesterday.

For example, we might react intensely to some minor irritation as if our world is crashing down on us. When taking a step back, we may realize that these strong emotions are stemming from a traumatic event that occurred in the past, which has not been addressed or resolved. We may have ignored it or been told not to talk or think about it.

Another reaction when these stress hormones are released is that they cause us to freeze or numb us, which might make our day-to-day events more of a struggle to connect with. For instance, we could feel emotionally detached during our child's birthday party or in response to the death of a loved one. As a result of not being able to fully take in what's going on around us, we might feel alienated and disconnected from our community.

Van der Kolk states that the solution to this problem is learning to identify our feelings and emotions and beginning to share them with a trusted friend or family member. By doing so, we learn to better manage our internal sensations and emotions, which brings us to the next lesson.

Lesson 4: We Have the Power to Regulate Our Physiology—Our Brain/Body Functions

Since our brain activity has been impacted

by trauma, our brainwaves are less coordinated than they should be. We then live out of our emotions and feelings, and not out of a carefully co-ordinated, thoughtful pattern of living. The good news is that dys-regulated brainwave patterns can be repaired; they can be rewired and transformed thanks to a process called *neuroplasticity*.

Neuroplasticity refers to the brain's ability to change, heal, or rewire itself in response to the stimulation of learning and healthy experiences. The brain has the ability to create new neurons (nerve cells in the brain) and connections between existing neurons throughout our lifetime. Neuroplasticity describes the way the brain has the special lifetime ability throughout to change, adapt, learn, and recover. It explains how our experiences can reorganize and develop new neural pathways in the brain. When we learn new things or memorize new information, we create lasting changes in the structure of our brain. It's like a muscle: the more we use or stretch it, the more powerful and helpful it becomes to our ways of thinking and functioning in the world.

Neuroplasticity allows neurons and the connections they form with each other to compensate for injury and adjust their activities in response to new thoughts or changes in the environment. There are many new strategies to help our brains heal and repair itself. Brain training apps and new technologies such as neurofeedback can enhance brain healing and train our brains to regulate our brainwaves to achieve the desired brainwave state—allowing us to be more focused and calm.

When doing neurofeedback training with

Myndlift, for example, a movie or a video game is played while EEG technology measures your brainwave activity. Every time your brain reaches its "happy state" or optimal brainwave level, you receive positive feedback. Then that feedback not only earns you points, but it gives insight into your brain function—when it's in its optimal state and when it's not.

Over time, after consistent training and use of neurofeedback, your brain learns to regulate itself and reach its optimal brainwave state without the immediate reward. Then you begin to realize you are learning and find it easier to stay calm in stressful situations. You will respond differently to events, traumatic memories, or emotions that may have overwhelmed you previously. It's important to note that this type of brain training doesn't require deliberate control. In this brain rewiring process, all you have to do is be mentally focused and physically relaxed, allowing your brain to relax, do its work, and follow the feedback.

We can use interventions like this to begin to decode and transform our responses to trauma. We don't have to remain stuck due to the memory of the trauma event lodged in our body. We can begin to let it go. If I can learn to do this, you can too.

Lesson 5: Positive Relationships Are Fundamental to Our Well-Being

Van der Kolk states in his book that our attachment bonds are our greatest protection against threats. Nothing soothes our fear like a soothing, calm, "safe" voice or a solid caring-felt hug from a trusted person. For instance, children who experience a traumatic event and are not immediately soothed by their parents or receive other forms of emotional support may suffer the effects of their trauma for a long time. In other words, traumatized human beings recover in the context of relationships, usually with families and loved ones. Alcoholics Anonymous meetings, Sexaholics Anonymous, veterans' organizations, religious communities, or professional therapists all serve to provide this kind of personalized support.

The purpose of healthy, trusting, safe relationships is to create and reinforce the bravery to accept, face, and process the reality of what has happened while offering physical and psychological safety and protection—especially safety from feeling shamed, admonished, or judged. Because we were made for relationships, when loving, caring relationships are not present to restore us to safety, peace, and calm, we can create them on our own. And when we do, we can often settle for inappropriate forms of relationships. We reduce ourselves to get a touch or hug any way we can, from anyone, and not all of them may be healthy or appropriate.

What I have learned and what has become so clear to me from my training, and reinforced when I teach or coach others, is that negative and acted-out destructive behavior are people's language of unmet needs, people who lost their voice to traumatic and often horrific life events. Giving a nonjudgmental voice to people is foundational to earning their trust, restoring their voice, and beginning their healing process. Relationships are vital to the healing of trauma. Nonjudgmental places or organizations, and people who can offer love and support, will greatly help others regulate their behavior and reduce their anxiety and related symptoms.

Van der Kolk says that when we have a persistent, aching sense of heartbreak and gut-wrenching pain, the physical sensations in our body become intolerable, and we will do anything to make those feelings go away. And that is the origin of what happens in human mental illness. People take drugs to attempt to make the pain disappear. They cut themselves to make it disappear. They starve themselves to make it disappear. And they have sex with anyone who comes along to make it disappear. They drink too much alcohol, smoke too much weed or crack, or ingest anything to attempt to make the pain go away. Once you have these horrible body sensations, you will do anything to make it fade, make it go away—even if only for a few minutes.

Simply put, trauma reshapes your brain, and it continues to grow and develop that way. It also helps coping mechanisms become habits, so they eventually are simply the way you do things and thus you are often unaware you are doing anything different from anyone else. I can't give you advice specific to your situation, but I can help you recognize the worst advice you can receive. Don't listen to anyone who tells you to just forget the past, live for today, or try to overcome it through sheer willpower.

You can't easily overcome who you are. You can't clean out your subconscious of everything you don't want, and you can't go back to being a child and relearn everything (you may have to do just that, but that occurs through therapy). It—whatever the "it" is—keeps resurfacing because it's become part of who you are. You were shaped and molded through one childhood and one life. You can change a lot of behaviors, but it takes time to realize what's happening and how you should instead be and respond. It takes time, but it can be done. I know that to be true because I did it.

CHAPTER 6
RESTORING YOUR VOICE

SUMMARY

- Trauma often silences people, making them feel their thoughts or emotions don't matter.
- Healing involves reclaiming your voice—learning to express needs, feelings, and boundaries with confidence.
- Speaking truth, especially in safe and supportive spaces, is a vital step toward self-worth and emotional freedom.

REFLECTIONS

- When have you felt unheard or unable to express what you really felt?
- How comfortable are you today sharing your thoughts and needs with others?
- What small steps can you take to use your voice more confidently and authentically?

CHAPTER 7

EFFECTS OF PRENATAL STRESS

"Curiosity opens the door to brilliance, inviting insights and discoveries within."
– Emily Wells

In this chapter, I want to share how pre-birth stress and related conditions can shape a child before the first breath is taken. As I noted earlier, the late Dr. Karyn Purvis once declared, "The most dangerous place for children is in utero." Her point was not to frighten us, but to focus our attention because we don't often consider a baby's prenatal environment and its lifelong consequences. Too often, this science and truth have not reached mainstream understanding, and we underestimate how profoundly important a mother's healthy body, mind, and surroundings are in preparing a child for the world to come.

A healthy pregnancy is more than a medical

event; it is a critical brain-body foundation. When a mother has adequate nutrition, hydration, rest, and emotional stability, she is building the child's ability to cope and survive in a healthy way. When stressors flood her body—substances like alcohol, nicotine, and drugs; poor diet; disrupted sleep; or chronic anxiety—those inputs alter the conditions in which the fetus grows. That is why meaningful, high-quality prenatal care matters for every mother and is especially critical for those with limited means. Attention to prenatal health improves outcomes at birth and supports growth and development into childhood and far beyond.

Obstetrics, which is the study of early child development and childbirth, has taught us that what happens in the womb does not stay in the womb. The unborn baby's environment inside the mother can influence the baby's long-term health. This perspective helps explain certain challenges that otherwise appear only after delivery. When we look for the roots of later difficulties—behavioral, emotional, or physiological—we must ask how development might have been shaped by conditions inside *and* outside the womb.

Stress to a baby before birth can be damaging. A mother's stress can change the baby's body in ways that directly influence her unborn child, or it can indirectly shape development by affecting the health of the pregnancy itself. Research indicates that ongoing maternal stress of the mother is not held only by the mother; it is often shared with the baby she carries. That sharing shows up later in the child's body and behavior. Ongoing work continues to clarify the mechanisms (how this happens), including how race, culture, environment, and heredity interact, and how experiences can alter how it is expressed across generations.

Not all stress is equal, but all stress matters. The range runs from severe events—trauma—to moderate transitions, such as a move or job change, down to daily hassles that accumulate. Early studies sometimes minimized these effects; the importance of later research points in a different direction: mild, moderate, and severe stress can all negatively influence pregnancy outcomes and the child's behavioral and physiological development. In short, "prenatal stress" is not one thing, because the stressors mothers face are not one thing.

Pregnancy often brings a second layer of concern—worries that are specifically about the pregnancy and the baby's well-being. That worry is understandable; it is also potentially dangerous. When a woman is anxious or fearful—even at conception—her body releases cortisol and adrenaline. The first systems to develop in an unborn baby are the brain and nervous system, so those chemicals are teaching the child's earliest wiring how to respond to the world. In that sense, the child can be "practicing" stress before ever being held. This may also clarify old labels like "colic," when some infants are in fact born with elevated stress hormones that complicate sleep, feeding, and digestion.

It is also important to acknowledge how social realities make their way into biology. Conception under coercion, fear, or shame—because of sexual violence, racial stigma, family pressure, or instability—floods a mother's body with stress she did not choose. That stress does not politely wait outside the womb. Without the mother ever intending it, anxiety can be shared with the baby, who then enters the world already sensitized to threat. That is not destiny, but it is a head start in the wrong direction and a call for early, compassionate support.

Let me make this more clear. Consider the everyday stressors a pregnant mother might face—housing insecurity, the grind of making ends meet, a relationship in turmoil, an unwanted pregnancy, or the fatigue of carrying too much too many other issues without sufficient support. Add to that the other biological stressors—alcohol, nicotine, and other drugs—all of which introduce chemicals that interfere with the baby's brain and nervous-system development. Put together, these forces amount to a steadily rising tide the child is swimming in. It is not surprising that we sometimes see the effects soon after birth in sleep disruption, difficulty self-soothing, or a heightened startle response.

This is where public health and justice meet. If we want healthy children, we must care for their mothers—medically, emotionally, and socially. Prenatal care is health care, but it is also prevention. It reduces risk for complications, improves birth outcomes, and sets the stage for healthy growth. For low-income and marginalized communities, appropriate access to care is not a luxury; it is the difference between building resilience and perpetuating harm across generations.

Understanding prenatal stress also reframes how we interpret early behavior. A hard-to-soothe infant may not be "difficult"; they may be overstimulated, their nervous system already trained to be on guard. Feeding issues may reflect not only digestion immaturity, but also the aftershocks of a stress-primed system. When we respond to children, especially those with challenging starts, with patience, structure, and consistent nurturance, we are helping re-teach their bodies what "safe" feels like.

With this insight, I understood the reason I was colicky as a baby. Perhaps my mom was anxious and nervous in those early moments of my being. Maybe during her pregnancy, she was anxious or even afraid of my dad, as she said she was when I asked her why she allowed him to close me up in the dresser drawer.

With this ongoing new scientific information, there is so much more I would like to ask her. There should be no more secrets. We should be willing to ask our parents and others about those precious nine months of pregnancy. And like me, you should ask yourself how you learned to be anxious and fearful. We accept our thinking and feelings without challenging them, even though some of them are unwanted guests that take up permanent residence in our being. We should come to a place where we stop and ask the deeper, harder questions. We are not the sum of our thoughts or feelings. Our thinking and feelings may be the result of how we came to be in our mother's womb.

A note about language: when I write about stress and pregnancy, I am not assigning blame to mothers. To the contrary, I am arguing for seeing the whole picture so that mothers get the support they deserve. Many women carry children while carrying burdens they did not choose. Our task is to reduce those burdens and surround them with care, not to shame them for what they have endured.

The science of epigenetics offers another window. Experiences—nutrition, stress, toxins—can influence how genes are expressed without changing the genes themselves. Think of it as adding bookmarks to a book: the words are the same, but which pages you open and re-read changes the story you live. There is emerging evidence that such changes can influence how future generations respond to stress. That should sober us, but it should also encourage us, because epigenetic marks can be responsive to improved environments, better nutrition, therapeutic support, and healthy relationships.

Let's pull the threads together. Trauma does not begin at age five or fifteen. For many, it begins before birth. A mother's chronic anxiety, a household roiled by conflict, food insecurity, or substance use—each of these can tune a developing brain toward vigilance. The good news is that development does not stop at birth. Brains remain plastic—capable of change—when we provide the right inputs: safe relationships, predictable routines, healthy nutrition and hydration, opportunities for movement and rest, and caregivers who regulate themselves while they help regulate their children.

What, then, should we do? First, elevate prenatal care for all mothers and remove barriers to access. Second, expand trauma-informed education for clinicians, social workers, teachers, and faith leaders so that prenatal and postnatal support are aligned. Third, invest in community supports that reduce the everyday stressors families face—housing, food, transportation, childcare—because those are health interventions, too. Fourth, communicate early and often that a mother's emotional well-being is health care for the child she carries. Fifth, design postpartum follow-up that continues the work of regulation—helping families establish routines, sleep strategies, and support networks that lower stress on both sides of the crib.

If you are a mother reading this, please hear this: you are not the enemy and neither are your emotions. Stress is a signal, not a verdict. Ask for help early. Hydrate, nourish your body, rest when you can, and invite safe people into your circle. If you have a history of trauma, tell your providers so they can care for you with that knowledge in hand. If you are a partner, family member, pastor, or friend, be part of the safety net. Reduce the load you can reduce. Listen. Encourage. Drive to appointments. Cook a meal. Sit in silence. Your calm presence is a gift to two nervous systems at once.

Healthy mothers nurture healthy babies, and healthy babies grow into adults more capable of restoring their own brilliance. When we honor the power of the prenatal environment and match that understanding with practical support, we do more than reduce risk—we cultivate life. That is the hope of this chapter and the invitation of the science: to see the child in the womb as already learning, already becoming, and to make every effort to let that learning happen in peace.

CHAPTER 7
EFFECTS OF PRENATAL STRESS

SUMMARY

- A mother's physical and emotional health during pregnancy directly affects her baby's brain and body development.
- Stress, fear, or trauma during pregnancy can influence a child's long-term ability to regulate emotions and handle life's challenges.
- Supporting mothers with care, rest, nutrition, and emotional safety is one of the best ways to break cycles of trauma before they begin.

REFLECTIONS

- How does understanding prenatal stress change the way you view early human development?
- What can families, communities, and churches do to better support expectant mothers?
- In what ways can you contribute to creating calmer, more supportive environments for both mothers and children?

CHAPTER 8

THERE'S HEALING IN SILENCE

"The journey to success is illuminated by the brilliance of your passion and drive."
– Leah Roberts

When my wife was diagnosed with breast cancer, I was shocked as was the rest of our family. Like many unexpected events in life, it came out of the blue, especially since her health had always been great. We had a wonderful marriage and a beautiful family. Even after we got married, we continued to court and date each other as friends. Our marriage was based on friendship. It was the core of our relationship.

After her diagnosis rocked our world, some of my evangelical prosperity-and-faith-focused pastor friends asked me questions that came out of their perception that God may be upset or angry with me. They recommended books to read and suggested that I enhance my faith walk, believing that cancer was an aberration and that God wanted His people to prosper and be in good health. While their advice was well-intentioned, it was not the best way to support a friend in need. It added to my sense of being alone in that painful space.

All that noise from them and other voices was deafening. I couldn't hear God amidst the chatter about what I needed to do. During that time, I heard about a nearby Benedictine retreat and monastery, and I knew Benedictine monks took a vow of silence in their daily living arrangements. I had heard about it but couldn't fully comprehend how they could maintain silence in modern times.

Healing Silence

One weekend, I decided to follow a friend's suggestion to spend some quiet time at that monastery retreat center. I took some cassette tapes and a player to provide some background sound. After settling into my room, I put on some music. It wasn't loud, but the monks could hear it outside my door. Soon, a monk gently knocked on my door to inform me that "we have a vow of silence."

I apologized and said, "I'll turn the music down," thinking that might satisfy him.

"No, we have a vow of silence. No talking, no music."

Suddenly, I realized that silence meant silence. It was to be nothing but me—and God.

I had never spent time like that before. My prayer time always involved music and lots of spoken words. I used gospel and praise-and-worship music to get in the mood and create a space where I thought I could "hear from God." This had served me well, or so I thought, over the years. After getting in the spirit, I would get out my prayer list and pray for family, friends, and all the things that came to mind. This was my routine no matter how much time I had—half an hour, an hour, or more.

Without realizing it, my faith development was framed in an emotional response to pain and suffering. I approached my faith experience with what I thought I needed—an emotional experience, connecting that to my pain and to God.

I began a journey in the monastery that would transform me. It was there that I began to learn to sit and become comfortable in my pain. I began a journey of learning about me, listening to me, being with me, sitting with me. It was a seismic shift in my approach to life and my personal identity.

I also began a journey of letting go of my faith experiences that were based on rules, judgments, condemnation, and shame. It was as if I had to learn about God in a new way. This was a period in my life when true faith began to emerge—a naked faith that came to life during my great pain.

It no longer felt like I had a formula for how to reach or control God. My former formula had to die to bring new life. And when I stood in my suffering, my life began to bear fruit in ways that were far beyond my understanding or expectation. I was no longer trying to escape my pain; I accepted it as my teacher.

I repeatedly returned to the Benedictine monastery, not really knowing what I was learning or doing. I just knew that new life was forming, and a basic calm and peace were beginning to flow in me. In those early days, I did not have a language or a vocabulary for the experiences. I just knew I was being transformed little by little each time I went.

Once when I came home from a quiet weekend retreat, my wife said, "I don't know about that Catholic quiet retreat stuff. But what I do know is that when you return home, you're more peaceful and calmer." Her affirmation, coming from a woman who was facing cancer and death, was key to my continuing to learn and experience this new spiritual practice. I went as often as I could, sometimes for a day, two days, or even a weekend.

I went so often that one day a monk asked me why I came so often while we were walking together on one of the sidewalks. I paused to gather my thoughts to share and then told him my wife had stage four cancer, and I needed to hear from God.

When I said those words, we stopped walking. He turned to me and asked with tears in his eyes, "Can I walk with you in that pain?" He didn't tell me what book to read. He didn't say I lacked the faith to believe in my wife's healing. He didn't judge or condemn me in any way. His kindness deeply penetrated me.

This was not a response I had heard or witnessed at any time while growing up. No one in my circle had ever responded this way. I remember thinking that Catholics must know something about pain and suffering that I do not. And there was a peace about which I wanted to know more.

So, I continued my journey into silence and quietness. I began to realize some of the peace in my spirit that my wife sensed or felt was that I had stopped exerting effort to exercise my faith, trying to do things correctly to earn God's approval—or my wife's healing. I was learning to be still and quiet, and the added benefit was that I was learning who I was.

I was learning that I was disconnected from my true self. Even before my wife passed, I was living in a busy, demanding culture. Much if not all my busy-ness and demands were my own doing—seeking outside validation and affirmation as a high-functioning, high-achieving professional. I realized that I had been looking for love and acceptance and approval in all the wrong places. I concluded that I was not mentally or emotionally well.

It is common knowledge that the relentless pace of modern life, characterized by constant demands, technological saturation, and a focus on external achievements, makes it difficult to maintain a strong connection to one's inner self and emotions. And when "religious" fervor is added to all that, I was a man not just trying to earn his father's approval but working diligently to get God's approval.

Getting in touch with my inner self—my true self—has been one of my greatest achievements. I have quieted down the noise of low self-esteem that screamed I was not good enough, while perceiving others as "perfect" which I wasn't. It was in learning to sit in silence that I found me!

CHAPTER 8
GENERATIONAL TRAUMA

SUMMARY

- Trauma doesn't end with one generation; pain, fear, and coping patterns can be passed down through families.
- Understanding how history, culture, and family experiences shape behavior helps us break unhealthy cycles.
- Healing begins when individuals acknowledge inherited wounds and intentionally create new, healthier legacies.

REFLECTIONS

- What patterns—emotional, relational, or behavioral—do you see repeating in your family history?
- How have your parents' or grandparents' experiences influenced the way you respond to life's challenges?
- What new patterns or traditions would you like to start so future generations experience more healing and peace?

CHAPTER 9

YOUR SPIRITUAL LIFE

"Brilliance is not a destination; it's cultivated through the journey and persistent efforts."
– James Price

Almost everyone agrees that we are spiritual beings. As one of those beings, I yearned for a deeper spiritual relationship and connection with God, but I did not know how to achieve them. I was looking for spiritual practices that would not only impact my spirit but also had physical and mental health benefits—while revealing more about who God is.

Researchers have consistently found a positive connection between mental health and a vibrant spiritual life. For example, when Harvard's T. H. Chan School of Public Health and Brigham and Women's Hospital reviewed hundreds of studies in 2022, they found that people who participated in the life and practices of a religious or faith community tended to live healthier, longer lives. However, researchers cautioned that spiritual practices aren't always holistically beneficial. Sometimes they can lead to greater anxiety and other mental health challenges. But the effects were positive in most cases.

What are some of these practices or disciplines that may lead to a healthier, more balanced approach and mindset?

Spiritual Practices

Spiritual practices are any set of activities or actions performed regularly to promote spiritual growth and development. They can take many forms and are expressed in different ways across faith and spiritual traditions. Some examples of spiritual practices include:

- Meditation: breathing in and out while focusing on a word or phrase
- Journaling: writing down thoughts and reflections
- Gratitude exercise: writing about things you love and for which you are grateful in your life
- Chanting: singing a simple chant repeatedly
- Forgiveness practices: reflecting on who you need to forgive
- Yoga: an ancient practice that involves breathing exercises and body poses
- Walking in nature: taking a walk along a nature trail or sitting under a tree

- Prayer: praying for people and situations
- Sacred reading
- Fasting: not eating food for a set period (always check with a physician before embarking on any type of fast)
- Centering prayer
- Contemplation

Three Ways to Better Own Your Faith

People have many motivations for practicing their faith or religion. Sometimes it is for the good feelings they derive from their practice and at other times it is for the acceptance they gain from those on a similar path. But our overall goal should be to keep moving toward a more authentically "owned" faith, one that is a source of meaning. This journey begins with a conscious decision to seek a more personal, honest, open connection with God. If you feel such a need, here are three practices to help you begin:

1. **Center your faith on your relationship with God.** When you go to a place or location to practice your faith or you sit at home or a park to read about your faith, do so with a genuine desire to connect with the Divine. Our prayer and stillness ought to lead us to a more intimate relationship with God. Don't talk "at" God, but with God. Bring your complete self, your best focus into

your conversing, sincerely expressing your thoughts, fears, hopes, and gratitude.

2. **Seek understanding.** Spend time learning more about your faith through study and reflection. Being assertive and leaning into your faith can help you better integrate a more genuine faith into your everyday practice, as opposed to just "going with the crowd" on a certain day of the week. Read books that deepen your understanding of spirituality and help you grow closer to the Divine.
3. **Seek spiritual direction.** Find a spiritual director or pastoral counselor who can help you identify hidden assumptions, old hurts, and patterns of behavior that may be preventing you from growing close to God. Choose one carefully and seek recommendations from others of people who have effectively served as guides in their faith walk.

When I learned to sit in silence, I began to realize that God had been waiting for me to sit with Him. He was eager to share truth nuggets of life's wisdom. I began to hear the birds sing differently, see sunrises and sunsets differently. I began to see the order in life and the order of things around me.

I began to find my brilliance!

CHAPTER 9
THE POWER OF AWARENESS

SUMMARY

- Healing starts with awareness—recognizing how past experiences influence present thoughts, feelings, and actions.
- Self-awareness allows us to pause before reacting, giving space to choose growth instead of repeating old patterns.
- Awareness leads to responsibility; once we see the truth, we can begin to change what no longer serves us.

REFLECTIONS

- What recurring emotions or reactions in your life might be connected to past experiences?
- When was the last time you paused to notice what you were feeling before responding?
- How can greater self-awareness help you make choices that bring peace and wholeness?

CHAPTER 10

MOVING FORWARD

"Discovering yourself is the key to unlocking the days of brilliance that await you."
– Piper Long

There is a lot of advice available on how to break old habits and establish new ones. Whatever the prescriptions, they seem to have one thing in common. They agree that it will take time to develop a new behavior when an old one is firmly entrenched.

When bad eating habits, stress, and/or anxiety have taken hold in my life, my focus should not be on the bad habits I want to break. It does me no good to stare at the ditch I am trying to avoid. Instead, my focus should be on the good, new habits I want to instill in their place. I need to keep my eyes on where I want to go and what I want to be. I move toward what I focus on—and so do you. The more often I repeat a certain action or think a certain thought, the more deeply it becomes ingrained in my brain.

Some years ago, I gave up eating beef and pork. I had high cholesterol, and I begged my doctor to allow me to try and lower it myself before he "forced" me to take prescription drugs to lower it. It was hard at first because I loved a good, greasy hamburger. But the longer I refused to stop at a hamburger restaurant, the easier it became to avoid it. A month later I went back to my doctor's office for a follow up visit, and my cholesterol had dropped. He said whatever I was doing to keep it up and come back in a month to see if the results held. I continued to avoid eating beef and pork, and each time I went back, my cholesterol had dropped. I learned then that repeating an action like avoiding red meat became easier over time and I had a new eating habit.

Therefore, repetition is the key to developing a new habit because repetition is how the old habit was developed in the first place. I must do all in my power to ensure I repeat the actions and thoughts of the desired good habit. The more I stay focused on that good path, the more the old undesirable path will fade.

But it all starts with changing yout focus. Don't fixate on the bad habit. You also need to determine what the opposite good habit is and focus on cultivating and nourishing that.

The same was true when I was trying to establish silence in my life. I found it hard at first to sit in silence. The more I did it, however, the easier it became. Now I miss my silent spaces if I have to skip a day or two. It's remarkable how much I now depend on silent spaces to settle down, sit still, breathe in, exhale, and to simply be with myself. It has become easier to accomplish a silent moment or many moments. I am now hooked.

How to Heal and Transform Your Life Every Day

Here is my last tip on how to successfully navigate this journey. Personal growth is a lifelong process, and it's one that I'm passionate about. I've been on this journey for years now, and I've discovered that the secret to success is taking small, daily steps towards my goals. It's not about making huge, sweeping changes overnight—it's about building positive habits and gradually becoming the person I want to be.

Are you ready to join me on this journey? If so, let me share some of the effective strategies I've found for improving yourself every single day. Before we move on, let me give you some background on the list. And the list is long and comprehensive, so I will divide it into two chapters.

When you get to the list, you will find it includes recommendations for sleep, exercise, diet, and hydration. I could easily list them together under a healthy living title, but they need and deserve their own section. People like me who have struggled with trauma anxiety have brains that need to be completely rewired. That means good nutrition and health are essential because they were part of my problem when they were unregulated. The body in stress craves salt, sugar, caffeine, starch—everything that is no good for us. The nervous and anxious body wants and needs healthy substances, but our brains have been sabotaged to think it wants the unhealthy instead of the healthy.

Also, we often do not live in a wholistic healthy space. How many times have you gone to your doctor's office and were asked to bring a record of your sleep patterns, your diet list for the past month, your exercise plan, and how much water you drink daily? They don't ask these things. Instead, they will prescribe medications that the body does not need to heal itself. In this modern era, we could learn from our ancestors that processed food is not good for us. So, I will focus on these one by one to raise your awareness and to encourage you to take each one of these on this list seriously. Let's get started.

1. Practice daily moments of quiet, peace, silence, meditation—no activity.

We live in a noisy and busy culture. I have learned to create regular *daily* space for being quiet and listening to my body, intellect, emotions, and spirit. I thought I knew these parts of me, but I did not. They were neglected, and I would frantically run around trying to get my schedule and my emotions under control. A regular, daily spiritual practice of mindfulness or meditation will profoundly improve your everyday life. These practices help you develop a sharper focus and also remain calm under stress. By incorporating prayer and mindfulness or meditation into your daily routine, you can:

- gain better control over your emotional reactions.
- increase your awareness of the present moment.
- improve concentration and reduce your day-to-day anxiety. This doesn't

require hours of practice each day; even a few minutes can make a significant difference.

- obtain better direction for your daily life which in turn will lead to a more fulfilling existence.

Create time each day for spiritual practices. You cannot grow unless you learn to sit in your pain, sit with yourself, and connect with your unknown, unloved self.

2. Get enough sleep.

When you are on a healing, restorative, transformational journey, remember that you must work with your total self—your entire body—to get this work done. You are part of a generation that is disconnected from your body. When I speak about being connected to our body so we know what it needs, some look at me as if this is modern pop psychology.

Previous generations had fewer external distractions and were more aware of their body's needs and message. We must learn to reconnect and cooperate with our body for our complete healing. This is not just a head or intellectual journey. Your unrelenting pain, anxiety, and stress reside in our body, not in your brain. So, you must not only heal your spirit, but you must also work to heal your body, and that begins by working with, observing, and giving this precious and highly efficient "machine" the care it needs.

The first step in this journey is getting enough sleep for both your physical and mental health. Adequate sleep plays a significant role in your healing, daily performance, and overall life quality. Adults should aim for 7-9 hours of sleep per night to function at their best.

Lack of sleep leads to poor concentration, mood swings, and decreased motivation, all of which hinder personal improvement endeavors. The memory system in our computer-like brain does not function properly when we do not get enough sleep. We cannot recall the details we need when our brain and body are tired and restless.

It is critically important that you make it a high priority to get good sleep by setting a consistent bedtime and creating a restful environment free from distractions like bright screens and noise. Turn off your phone, TV, or other devices an hour or so before going to sleep. Let your brain and body begin to transition into a rest mode before jumping into bed.

3. Maintain a healthy diet.

From my own personal experience and from coaching others, people who are stressed, anxious, and full of fear often crave unhealthy food. We crave salt, sugar, and carbohydrates—all the substances that negatively impact our health when we most need good health. We are stressed and overweight. We are stressed and tired. We are stressed and depressed.

To help with this process, try this: Keep a daily tab of what you eat for an entire week and see what I mean. Be honest with yourself and see how unhealthy your intake is. Eating unhealthy foods enhances your anxiety and depression. You must work with your body for your total healing.

Eating well is not only about avoiding illness; it's about strengthening your mind and body for the work of healing from your personal issues. A healthy diet fuels your body for daily activities and, after even a short time, will significantly boost your mood and energy levels.

To maintain a healthy diet:

- Include a variety of vegetables and fruits in your daily meal diet.
- eliminate cookies, cakes, and pies and instead turn to whole grains and lean proteins like grilled chicken and fish.
- limit the intake of sugar, salt, and saturated fats.

Gradually, you will see that your dietary habits provide the necessary nutrients to fuel and support both your physical activities and your brain and cognitive tasks, enabling you to pursue your daily self-improvement goals more effectively. And you will sleep better and begin to go about your day with less stress and anxiety. (Don't stop taking any meds without consulting with your doctor.)

4. Drink plenty of water.

We are a dehydrated generation. We don't drink enough water daily. When we are stressed, many of us crave other liquids, but not water. Our taste buds change when we are anxious and stressed. And when our bodies appear to want food or other items, it is screaming for water. Our bodies need water in every part of our body. Our unique, wonderful brain sits in a thin film-like substance that has a liquid water-like content. When our bodies are dehydrated, our brains are probably dehydrated also. When that occurs, we don't think well. We don't function well. We are not clear-headed.

When it comes to healing and living and operating in your best self, hydration is often the unsung hero—especially as you age. That's why I place a special category for hydration in this list. Working through my own personal challenges and observing my family, myself, and those I coach and support, I've seen firsthand how small changes like staying properly hydrated have a huge impact on energy, focus, and overall well-being.

At this stage of my life, I want to focus more on helping people, young and old, unlock their full potential through proper hydration and nutritional strategies. It's not just about drinking more water; it's also about finding the right balance of fluids and nutrients to support good brain health, muscle strength, bone growth, and proper blood flow as your body changes and matures.

Begin the day with an eight-ounce glass of water. Your body is dehydrated from a good night's sleep, and you usually wake up groggy, sluggish, and not clear-headed. All of this contributes to and impacts your anxious state. This will also help your digestive system work effectively. Drink water before your first cup of coffee, and then drink water all day. Learn to become aware of your hydration signals. There are several good apps to help you keep track of your daily water intake. Please take this seriously. Water hydration is important to your overall mental and physical health.

5. Accept yourself as you are.

After finding time each day to be quiet and peaceful, I learned that I needed to respond to the negative voice that kept interrupting my quiet time. To improve yourself every day, one of the first things to do is to start accepting yourself exactly as you are and where you are on your journey. No matter your story or journey, you are a gift to the planet. And you can't love others if you don't love yourself. If you are looking for someone to love you, they can't love you until you love and accept yourself. This means you should begin to acknowledge both your strengths and weaknesses without judgment. When you accept yourself, you begin to reduce your shame and set a stable foundation for growth.

This doesn't mean you stop striving to be and do better, but instead you recognize that self-care and self-improvement come more smoothly when you are not fighting against your own negative self-talk and negative self-image. When you accept you and where you are, this reduces internal conflicts that can block personal progress.

Today make a commitment to self-compassion. You may have to do this every day for a month—or longer. You may have a deep self-hatred that clouds your view of yourself and your world. If you don't see yourself as God sees you, then these are empty words, and you end up saying, "Here's another book that doesn't help me." Self-compassion is critical to your transformation and your ability to move on from the pain that was delivered to the door of your heart and mind.

6. Set your boundaries

Establishing clear personal boundaries is vital and essential for creating healthy self-development. Boundaries help you define what you need in your garden to grow and how you want to be treated by others. Setting clear boundaries supports your mental health and conserves your emotional energy by protecting you from being overwhelmed or taken advantage of by others. Remember, there is nothing wrong with making your needs your highest priority!

When setting boundaries:

- clearly and kindly communicate your needs and limitations to those around you.
- be consistent in maintaining these boundaries.
- remember that it's permissible to say no when something doesn't align with your values or current capabilities.
- at each success, don't just move on—celebrate with yourself. Take a few minutes to say quietly and peacefully to yourself how proud you are that you were able to keep your boundaries. Celebrate you!

7. Stay active.

Regular physical activity is a key to improving yourself every day. One of the significant benefits of daily exercise is that it helps manage stress and anxiety and boosts your energy and endurance levels. You don't need intense workouts to stay active; simple activities like walking, jogging, cycling, swimming, or skating can be highly beneficial. Aim for at least 30 minutes of moderate exercise most days of the week and more when you feel stressed. Staying active can also enhance your mental clarity and emotional stability, making it easier to tackle nagging daily challenges and growth opportunities.

8. Spend time outdoors.

Spending more time outdoors in the fresh air and sun is not only refreshing but also beneficial for your mental and physical health and here's why. Exposure to natural sunlight boosts vitamin D levels, which is crucial for bone health and immune function. When you leave your smart phone inside, being without it provides an opportunity to disconnect from distractions and engage in physical activity, whether it's walking, cycling, or just enjoying a quiet moment in a park. Disconnecting from mindless activity like TV and phones regularly and immersing yourself in nature can improve your mood, increase your energy levels, and enhance your overall sense of well-being.

9. Limit activities, events, and people that drain you.

To improve every day, it's crucial to identify and limit activities that drain your energy without providing significant benefits, especially early in your recovery or transformation. This could involve slowly reducing time spent on social media, not watching your favorite TV show, or backing down from spending time with your group at a club or bar. It could also be reducing time spent with friends or family members that drain the life out of you. You have permission to say, "not now." There may be an opportunity soon or at another time for your interaction with them.

By freeing up and prioritizing more quality time and energy for you, you can focus on activities that enhance your well-being and contribute to your personal growth. The intent here is to live in those spaces that feed, support, and nourish you. Surrounding yourself with positive people and activities is critical to maintaining your motivation to keep moving forward because negative people can drain your energy and distract you from your goals.

10. Watch and listen to positive media.

Filling your day with positive media can significantly influence your mood and outlook. Pay attention to how much of what you listen to is negative or not producing a positive outcome. When you stop watching and listening to negative things, you will see a major difference in your mood and attitude. Listening to inspirational stories or uplifting podcasts reinforces positive mental habits and perspectives that support your personal growth. This could be as simple as choosing TV or video shows or dramas that motivate, music that uplifts, or productions that teach something valuable. Make a conscious choice to consume content that enhances positivity in your life, helping you maintain the push and drive to stay motivated daily.

To protect your mental well-being, it's important to:

- recognize patterns of negativity in relationships.
- set boundaries with individuals who consistently bring negativity into your life.
- seek out and nurture relationships, activities, and events with those who encourage and uplift you.

11. Develop a way to express yourself.

Finding your unique voice and expressing yourself clearly are vital for personal growth. This could take the form of writing, painting, music, adult coloring books, or even coding. You may have an inclination toward art but expressing yourself isn't just about the art—it's about finding ways to communicate your inner thoughts and feelings. When you develop music, writing, or other communication skills, you're able to convey your talents and desires more effectively, enrich your relationships, and increase your self-esteem. Practice a method of artistic expression that feels right for you and notice the clarity it brings to your life and work.

12. Learn to say "NO."

Learning to say no may not be a big step for you, but it's a powerful step towards your own personal self-improvement. It involves recognizing and understanding your limits and prioritizing your well-being over pleasing others. Moving forward is about you speaking up for and doing what's best for you. Saying no can be difficult, especially if you're worried about disappointing people, but it's essential for managing your time and energy effectively.

Start small by saying no to requests and invitations that don't line up with your goals or values, and practice being firm yet respectful. This skill may not be comfortable at first, and it may drain your emotional energy, but learning to manage your no will help you stay true to your personal growth journey.

Let me stop here so you can process what you have read. When you are ready to continue, move on to the next chapter.

CHAPTER 10
THE IMPORTANCE OF SAFETY

SUMMARY

- Feeling safe—physically, emotionally, and spiritually—is essential for healing and healthy relationships.
- People who have lived with fear or instability must often relearn what safety feels like and how to trust it.
- Creating safe environments, both within ourselves and with others, allows growth, connection, and restoration to take root.

REFLECTIONS

- What environments or people help you feel most at peace and secure?
- How do you know when you're beginning to feel unsafe or anxious, and how do you respond?
- What can you do to build a sense of safety for yourself and those around you?

CHAPTER 11

THE LIST CONTINUED

"Embrace personal growth as an adventure, leading to the brilliance that awaits within."
–Jason Mitchell

You're doing well if you have gotten this far. Remember, what I am sharing is not a laundry list. It's a menu of things that you can work on at any given point in your life. I hope there are a few that literally jump off the page at you, which is a sign those are where you need to start. As you gain confidence, you can move on to other areas. As I write, I am seventy years old, so I have accumulated this list over time, and I am sharing it with you now so you can hopefully start earlier than I did and be in a better place than I was when you reach my age. Let's continue.

13. Do the inner work.

The daily journey to improve yourself isn't complete without doing what is called inner work. This involves self-reflection so you can understand your emotions, values, and thought patterns, and see where any problems or challenges may exist. This process can help identify the root causes of your nagging pain, fears, and unhappiness that you may have suppressed and pushed down in your inner being.

Remember, the work you're doing is about getting away from your nagging negative feelings. Techniques such as journaling, meditation, or talking with a therapist or a trusted mentor or coach can facilitate this kind of deep self-exploration. Making personal time for significant inner work is essential no matter how uncomfortable it is. It gets you in touch with who you are behind and beyond all the trauma and rage. It also lays the mental and emotional foundation necessary for sustained personal growth so you don't pass on your pain to future generations!

14. Acknowledge your flaws.

Improving yourself includes not only recognizing your strengths but also acknowledging your flaws. This doesn't mean you are hard on yourself; it's about recognizing areas where you can grow. By honestly seeing and owning your weaknesses, you can better target your self-improvement efforts. This might include working on skills where you don't feel as confident or developing habits that have hindered your progress. Recognizing and understanding your issues leads to a more grounded and realistic path toward growth. I am not implying this will be easy or fun. We all have areas in our lives that we need to see, own, and rework.

15. Confront your fear of failure.

Everyone fears failure, but overcoming this fear is critical for daily improvement. To begin confronting your fear of failure, start by defining what failure looks like for you. Understand that missteps or poor performance are normal and often provide valuable lessons. Here's how you can begin to reduce fear daily:

- challenge yourself by performing small tasks that push you out of your comfort zone.
- reflect and journal what you learned from each experience, not just the outcome.
- gradually increase your challenges as you create and build confidence from your successes and lessons learned. And pay attention to how you begin to feel.

This process helps you transform fear and anxiety into a motivational tool rather than a barrier and hindrance to your success. You also begin to create new neuropathways in your brain, rewiring it for health and well-being.

16. Never stop learning.

Continuing to learn is another vital part of daily self-improvement. The world around you is always changing, so keeping up-to-date with new information and skills can open doors to opportunities and personal growth. Make it a daily goal to learn something new every day, whether it's a small thing, or a complex concept, or a life skill.

A never-stop-learning mindset not only enhances your knowledge base but also keeps your mind sharp and engaged. It is part of being curious about yourself and the whole world around you. And you will begin to activate parts of your brain that want to learn more every day.

17. Stop a bad habit and cultivate a new one.

Learning new habits daily or often is a powerful routine for self-improvement. Start with small, easy changes that may bring a sense of accomplishment to your new routine. For example, you might decide to read for 15 minutes before bed or to start your mornings with a ten-minute meditation. Consistency is key, so stick with your new habit every day until it becomes second nature. This step helps you create new brain waves that become "habits" of discipline. Then stand back and watch as new habits begin to change various aspects of your life, from health to productive outcomes.

18. Adopt a new hobby, new schedule, new friends.

Engaging in a new hobby can be fun and enriching at the same time. It allows you to explore new ideas, develop new skills, meet new people, and open up doors you did not know existed in you or in the world. Whether it's gardening, painting, or learning a musical instrument, hobbies provide a creative outlet and can relieve stress. New hobbies offer you a chance to challenge yourself in a new and exciting way, which is great for personal development. You may discover a new hidden talent. Don't worry about perfection right away; enjoy the learning process and the journey of exploring something new.

19. Try a new routine or schedule.

Changing your daily or weekly schedule and routine can lead to significant improvements in productivity and personal satisfaction. If you find yourself stuck in a rut doing the same things and not getting anything done, changing your routine might help. Look at different times to do things you normally do or change up the way you have usually done things to see what new rhythms might begin to feel comfortable. For example, if you have more energy in the morning, schedule your most demanding tasks in the morning, or if you are an evening person, try the evening for your demanding task. Remember, flexibility is key. Do not get locked into a new routine until you feel like it fits you.

20. Let go of the past.

Letting go of your past mistakes, issues, and failures—or whatever holds you back—can be one of the most liberating steps towards improvement. Holding onto regrets or past mistakes can cloud your current judgment and slow down your growth. Focus on what you can control in the present and here's how:

- acknowledge past experiences and the lessons they provided, and say, "Yes, I messed that up. But I'm moving on!"
- consciously declare you are moving

forward without letting these experiences dictate your future decisions.

- use reflection statements like, "I'm learning from my past and I'll keep moving to bigger and better things." Be as specific as you can about what you want for yourself in your future. Remember each day offers a new opportunity for growth and learning.

21. Use your past experiences.

Your past experiences are valuable lessons, not just memories. Each experience, whether positive or negative, holds insights that can guide future decisions and strategies. To use these experiences constructively:

- regularly reflect on past situations and the outcomes they led to, but don't dwell on them. Just reflect on what happened and how you got there.
- identify the patterns in your behavior that got you there and think about how you can avoid those patterns in the future.
- daily apply these insights to similar situations and you will find the temptations lessening to repeat old behaviors.

This practice helps you avoid past mistakes and makes you more aware of how to move through your new life while boosting your personal development and self-esteem.

22. Follow your dreams and aspirations.

This step starts with clarity. What is it you really want for or out of your life? Be honest and specific about this. Setting clear, achievable goals based on your dreams can provide a roadmap to follow. This new plan will keep you motivated during tough times when you may want to quit. Regularly revising and reminding yourself of these goals ensures that your daily actions align with your long-term aspirations. You move toward what you dream about and imagine for your life. If you have no dream or goal, you are more likely to remain stuck and have no direction. Follow your dreams.

23. Create ways to meet new people.

Meeting new people may not be easy or exciting at first. But meeting them can open up a social network, bring fresh people into your life, and lead to opportunities for both personal and professional growth. To create ways to meet new people, consider joining clubs, classes, or groups that line up with your interests and dreams. Attending conferences or community events can also be a great way to connect with others who share your passion or career path.

Each new friend, guide, or acquaintance offers a potential window into different cultures, ideas, and practices that can enrich your understanding of the world and contribute to your self-improvement. Ask your coach or advisor if they have any ideas about how you can meet new people. However, when you think about it, we all have opportunities to meet new people—in the grocery store, at a sporting event, or at a department store.

24. Create ways to build long-lasting relationships.

You may need new friends and new relationships especially if the ones you have are hindering your growth. Building long-lasting relationships is more than just spending time together; it's about nurturing these connections through understanding, respect, and mutual support. Make time to listen actively to others and offer help without expecting anything in return, while consistently and openly communicating your thoughts and feelings. These actions develop trust and appreciation, which are vital for relationships that not only endure but are enriching and uplifting as well. Developing new, strong, mature relationships can significantly enhance your personal growth by providing emotional support and new perspectives. Believe me, you will need new trusted friends as you move away from your old life.

25. Identify mentors and coaches.

Having a mentor or a coach can dramatically increase your personal growth and development. Mentors provide support, guidance, motivation, and feedback based on their own experiences and achievements. To find a mentor, identify someone you admire in your community, and reach out to them with specific questions or requests for advice. Do not wait around for the other person to reach out to you. Be assertive in maintaining and building this new relationship by setting regular meetings or check-ins and coming prepared with updates on your progress and new questions. This relationship not only helps you learn faster but also provides you with a trusted blueprint for handling both successes and setbacks.

26. Plan your goals, and then make time to work on them.

I've mentioned this before, but I repeat it because it is important to your growth and development. Effective goal setting is a dynamic tool for personal improvement. Start by clearly defining what you want to achieve, breaking these aspirations into achievable tasks. Here's a simple way to keep your planning effective:

- write down your main goals.
- break each goal into smaller, manageable tasks.
- set deadlines for these tasks.
- schedule specific times in your week to focus on these tasks.

Consistently dedicating time to work on your goals helps turn your dreams into reality, fostering a sense of accomplishment and motivating you to keep pushing forward—even when you don't feel like much is going on, or you want to turn back to old unproductive thinking and behavior.

27. Boost your confidence.

Sometime in the process of discovering who you are and changing, you will need to build self-confidence. Improving your self-confidence is a fundamental part of self-improvement that affects every aspect of your life. It is a matter of constantly repeating certain activities. Confidence comes from a combination of self-awareness, preparation, and experience. To build your confidence:

- repeat any or all these guidelines.
- purposely take new challenges that push you out of your comfort zone.
- prepare thoroughly for tasks to reduce anxiety.
- celebrate small victories that reinforce your sense of accomplishment.

As you experience success, you will begin to feel a sense of accomplishment, your experiences will broaden, and your skills improve. You will wake up one day and realize that your confidence naturally developed and you may not have noticed.

At this point in your journey, having read through all these suggested steps and processes, it is important to resist the temptation to take on everything at once. I have given you a wide range of ideas, practices, and strategies, but remember growth happens when you pick one, two, three, or more steps and you stay steady and intentional with them. Choose just a few items that stand out to you—those that resonate most with your current needs or challenges—and commit to working on them consistently every day.

As you repeat these actions, they will become habits that take root, creating real change in your daily life. Remember, your brain creates new pathways when you consistently repeat behavior.

Then the behavior becomes a routine or habit. And when it's a habit, the old behavior and thinking may reappear, but you will resist it because you have new habits.

At the same time, guard yourself against doing too much too quickly. Overloading your plate may only lead to discouragement and slower progress. This is a marathon, not a sprint, and steady forward motion is what counts. Celebrate the small wins, be patient with yourself, and know that each step taken is a step in the right direction. Once you've made progress with a few habits, you'll have the confidence and energy to expand into others. For now, keep your focus clear, your steps simple, and your vision strong. That is how transformation unfolds.

Real progress begins with choosing a few clear steps and walking them out faithfully, one day at a time. That same principle applies not just to your habits, but to the deeper work of uncovering who you really are beneath the masks you have worn.

In the next chapter, we'll turn to that very challenge—learning how to take off the mask, face ourselves honestly, and discover the freedom that comes when we live authentically with ourselves and others.

CHAPTER 11
THE POWER OF FORGIVENESS

SUMMARY

- Forgiveness is a key step in healing—it frees you from the weight of anger, resentment, and bitterness.
- Choosing to forgive doesn't mean excusing harm; it means releasing the control the past has over your peace.
- True forgiveness is a process that begins in the heart and often takes time, courage, and support.

REFLECTIONS

- Who or what do you still need to forgive to find more freedom and peace?
- How does holding onto resentment affect your physical or emotional health?
- What might change in your life if you allowed forgiveness to reshape how you see the past?

CHAPTER 12

A SUMMARY AND THE WAY FORWARD

"Understanding oneself is the first step to unleashing personal brilliance." – James Taylor

As I mentioned in the Introduction, everyone has a story, and I have been sharing mine with you. Stories matter because they help us understand ourselves and the world we live in. Too often, I see people stuck in the pain of their past—resulting in fear, anxiety, and depression—because, like I did, they hold on to incomplete and distorted stories about who they are and where they came from. The story I have just told you is my journey of healing, transformation, and hope. It's about how I came to embrace my pain and use it to find freedom and purpose.

This book is especially for people like me—men who face unique challenges shaped by race, poverty, and generational trauma. I share openly about faith and spirituality because, like Joseph in the book of Genesis, I have come to believe that what was meant for harm, God can use for good. We've covered a lot of material, and I want to give you a concise summary of what we discussed along with some basic recommendations for you as you start or continue your own healing journey.

Growing Up: Mom and Dad

I've told you of being born in rural Oklahoma, the oldest of seven children. My parents were sharecroppers who struggled just to survive. My dad was emotionally distant—he grew up in a family and culture where affection was rare, especially for Black men of his generation. My mother was a loving cook and caretaker but carried her own quiet burdens.

My childhood was full of fear, anxiety, and strict discipline. Mom told me that I spent nights crying in a dresser drawer because we couldn't afford a crib. I was often punished harshly, and my father never told me he loved me. But I also understand now that their behavior was shaped by their own pain and the harsh realities they faced.

I regret not knowing more about my family's history—so many African Americans share this loss. Our ancestors' stories are often unknown, yet their trauma is passed down. That silence can bind us unless we seek healing.

Finding My Way: College and Early Adulthood

When I left home at 18 for Kansas State University, I was determined never to return to that painful chapter. I threw myself into school and leadership roles—so much so that I was called an overachiever. I became the first Black student body president there, an achievement I'm proud of but which also masked my inner wounds. My drive was fueled by a desperate need for approval.

After college, I pursued counseling degrees and found myself drawn to understanding the human mind and family systems. My work took me from academia to ministry, marriage, and fatherhood. But life's challenges—my wife's cancer, the loss of loved ones—pushed me into deeper reflection and growth.

Parenting and Healing

Adopting my daughter was a profound blessing but also a challenge. Her early life trauma, like so many adopted and foster children, required me to learn about attachment disorders and trauma-informed parenting. After my wife's death, I became a single father navigating my own healing while supporting her. I learned that trauma isn't always visible. Both of us carried deep wounds, but outwardly we appeared "fine." Healing was a daily process of patience, love, and learning.

Living with High-Functioning Anxiety

For many years, I was a textbook example of high-functioning anxiety—outwardly successful and organized, but internally battling constant worry, self-doubt, and the need to please. My childhood neglect left me with anxiety that fueled my workaholism and perfectionism.

I came to understand that anxiety is not just a mental challenge but also rooted in how our brains process stress and trauma. Accepting this, seeking help, and practicing mindfulness and self-care were essential steps in reclaiming peace.

Understanding Trauma through Neuroscience

One of the most powerful parts of my journey has been learning about trauma through brain science. Books like *The Body Keeps the Score* by Dr. Bessel van der Kolk opened my eyes to how trauma literally changes the brain and body.

Our brain's "smoke detector," the amygdala, becomes hypersensitive after trauma, keeping us on constant alert—even when the danger is gone. This leads to emotional reactivity, anxiety, and physical health problems. Trauma is stored in the body, and healing requires more than just willpower or "forgetting" the past.

But there is hope: our brains can rewire themselves through neuroplasticity. Through therapies like neurofeedback, mindfulness, and loving relationships, we can retrain our brains to find calm and safety.

The Power of Relationships in Healing

Healing doesn't happen in isolation. We were made for connection. Safe, supportive, and nonjudgmental relationships are fundamental to recovering from trauma. Whether it's family, faith communities, support groups, or therapy, being known and accepted helps us process pain and rebuild our sense of self.

Too often, people act out destructive behaviors because they have lost their voice and hope. Offering love and a safe space is the first step toward restoration.

Looking Back and Moving Forward

My story is a testament to the fact that our past does not have to define our future. Generational trauma may have shaped me, but it does not have to control me. Through faith, education, neuroscience, and community, I have found ways to heal and help others do the same.

Today, I work with young people caught in cycles of violence and despair, bringing the lessons I have learned into their world. My hope is that by sharing my journey, others will find the courage to face their pain, transform their stories, and step into the brilliance that is inside each of them.

What You Can Do Now: My Recommendations to You

If you've read this far, you may be wondering, "Where do I go from here? How do I start healing or help others?" Here are some practical steps I encourage you to consider—things that helped me and that I believe can help you, no matter where you are in your journey:

1. **Acknowledge Your Story and Pain**
   Begin by recognizing your own story, including the pain and trauma you carry. Don't minimize it or pretend it's not there. The first step to healing is honest awareness.
2. **Seek Safe Relationships**
   Find people—family, friends, counselors, or support groups—where you can share your story without fear of judgment. Healing happens in connection, not isolation.

3. **Practice Mindfulness and Stillness**
   Set aside daily time for quiet—meditation, prayer, or simple breathing exercises. These moments help calm the nervous system and allow your brain to rest and rewire.
4. **Educate Yourself about Trauma and Healing**
   Learning about how trauma affects the brain and body can empower you to understand your reactions and responses. Books like *The Body Keeps the Score* or working with trauma-informed professionals are excellent resources.
5. **Take Care of Your Body**
   Physical health supports mental and emotional healing. Eat nourishing foods, get enough sleep, exercise regularly, and limit substances that increase anxiety.
6. **Consider Professional Help**
   Therapists trained in trauma and attachment disorders can guide you in healing. Please do not be afraid to ask for help—it's a sign of strength, not weakness. We have all needed support along our journey. And consider asking for intensive therapy. A 50-minute session once a week may not be adequate. And if the professional suggests prescription drugs,

tell them you have had all the drugs you want. You want some life-giving solutions—now!

7. **Embrace Spiritual Practices if They Resonate**
   Whether through faith, prayer, meditation, or community worship, nurturing your spirit can provide deep comfort and guidance. For me, faith has been a cornerstone of healing.
8. **Please, Please Be Patient and Compassionate with Yourself**
   Healing is a journey, a day-by-day journey. We don't get to the finish line overnight. There will be good days and bad days. Celebrate progress, no matter how small, and forgive yourself when setbacks happen.
9. **Use Your Story to Help Others**
   When you're ready, sharing your journey can inspire and support others who are struggling. There is power in vulnerability and in transforming pain into purpose.

I encourage you to take one step today—whatever that looks like for you. You don't have to do it all at once. Healing is a journey, and every journey begins with a single step. If I can find freedom and purpose after years of pain, so can you.

CHAPTER 12
A SUMMARY AND THE WAY FORWARD

SUMMARY

- Healing is a lifelong journey of awareness, forgiveness, and growth—it unfolds one step at a time.
- Restoring your brilliance means reclaiming the strength, purpose, and peace that trauma tried to steal.
- Moving forward requires intentional choices: to seek help, to stay connected, and to live with compassion for yourself and others.

REFLECTIONS

- What have you learned through this journey that gives you new hope or direction?
- What practical steps can you take this week to continue your healing and growth?
- How can you use your story to bring encouragement or light to someone else's path?

FINAL THOUGHTS

When we step back, step into silence, and learn to listen, we quickly learn that God does not waste any of our experiences. He uses all things for our good, and sometimes for the good of others around us. This book has been a struggle to write and edit, but I am coming to see that when the author is ready, the spirit arrives and has helped me see my intentions for writing and what to focus on.

We are spiritual beings having an earthly experience, and it is more intense and confusing than ever. Even in our religious frameworks, we have a rigid head knowledge about our faith, but our heart is not involved, our spirit is not cultivated, and the deep spaces of pain and neglect crave to be soothed. Our pain is masked and covered up by the little we get from sitting in pews attending church, but church does not often penetrate our inward being and help us confront our sordid and painful histories and patterns. And some of us leave church feeling worse than when we first arrived.

As I close the final page of this book, I am eager to find a space of quiet. I am more in touch with my inner self where the Divine lives. I am more aware of who I am on this earth. I can watch and listen to the events of our day and not let that noise get to me because I have come to understand that all I have control over is me. I am cultivating a space each day to be calm and relaxed.

Sure, I can pray and meditate about the events around us. But again, at the end of the day, it's out of my control and my being anxious, nervous, pretending and looking good are not helping me be me. Those days are over. I want to stop and listen. To hear the care-free sparrows in their morning chorus or see a rabbit or squirrel hunt for food. I want to be quiet so I can hear the heavens speak to the deep parts of me, that I am more than good enough. I am brilliant—and so are you!

As you set off now with your brilliance, will you make a commitment to follow some of the suggestions in this book? Here are some affirmations and commitments you can make to get you started on your way. You don't have to embrace them all, but focus on one or two and when you make progress (and you will), come back and choose others to work on.

1. I recognize that curiosity is one of the secrets to unlocking my brilliance and I will read books about self-improvement and self-care.
2. I will take control of my personal self-care, my mental and physical health by eating healthy, drinking water daily, exercising, and getting enough sleep.
3. I will learn new techniques to manage my emotions, my anger, my

temper and how I respond to negative events in my life.

4. I will take time each day for silence, personal reflection and to be present in my spiritual practices to reflect on my thoughts and feelings. And I will journal these reflections often.
5. I will learn to actively listen to my body and mind, better understanding when I feel stressed, overwhelmed, bored, tired or lonely, and will develop healthy responses.
6. I am committed to daily being more aware of my brilliance and how I am a gift to humanity.
7. I will not give up pursuing my brilliance.
8. I am worthy of good things coming to me.
9. I will repeat positive affirmations daily.
10. I will not give up. I will not stop. I will reach my true brilliance. I am "Restoring Brilliance."

MORE BRILLIANCE QUOTES

In my research for quotes that pertain to brilliance, I found some I could not include in the manuscript, so I decided to include them here.

- "Brilliance emerges when we choose to explore the depths of our own truth."
  – Aubrey Adams
- "Understanding oneself is the first step to unleashing personal brilliance."
  – James Taylor
- "The journey of self-discovery unlocks hidden brilliance and a deeper vision of purpose."
  – Charlotte Wells
- "Embrace personal growth as an adventure, leading to the brilliance that awaits within."
  – Jason Mitchell
- "Your unique brilliance emerges when you align your values with your intentions."
  – Eva Reed
- "Self-discovery is a continuous journey, revealing the brilliance embedded within us all."
  – Zoe Hall

- "The path to brilliance is paved with the stones of self-reflection and growth."
  – Samuel Scott
- "Embrace change and watch your brilliance unfold; it is a part of your evolution."
  – Hannah Nelson
- "Brilliance lies not in perfection but in the courage to pursue growth and knowledge."
  – Ryan Foster
- "Discovering yourself is the key to unlocking the days of brilliance that await you."
  – Piper Long

Bernard holds an MS in Counseling and Behavioral Studies from the University of South Alabama and a Ph.D. in Counseling, Higher Education Administration, and Family Studies from Kansas State University. He completed Trust-Based Relational Intervention (TBRI®) Practitioner Training at TCU's Karyn Purvis Institute of Child Development. Bernard has participated in various trauma and neuroscience trainings with leading experts worldwide and has taught undergraduate courses in psychology and neuroscience. He is passionate about continually studying and keeping up with the latest research on the human brain and neuroscience.

CONTACT DR. BERNARD FRANKLIN

bfranklinphd@restoringbrilliance.org

www.restoringbrilliance.org

Restoring Brilliance, Inc.
PO Box 220073
Dorchester, MA 02122

Made in the USA
Coppell, TX
14 February 2026